What Every Child Should Know Along the Way

Teaching practical life skills
in every stage of life

Gail Martin

What Every Child Should Know Along the Way

Published by Parent-Wise Solutions, Inc.

Copyright 1998 by Gail Martin

International Standard Book Number: 1-932740-18-X

Printed in the United States of America

For information:
Parent-Wise Solutions, Inc.
2130 Cheswick Lane, Mt. Pleasant, SC 29466

04 05 06 **07** – 7 6 5 4 3 2 1

Dedication

This book is dedicated to
Jim, my wonderful husband and friend,
and to my children, Christopher, Jeremy, Jesse and Esther:
our gifts, rewards and blessings from God.

In Appreciation

I wish to extend my appreciation to:

My husband, Jim,
for his patient and enduring
help during this writing.

Dawn Shultz,
for her friendship, tireless editing,
suggestions, and encouragement.

My parents, Dr. John and Marjorie Merjanian,
who have loved me and raised me with many
of the principles written in this book.

Table of Contents

Foreward

⁂

I t is a great pleasure for me to write the Foreword to *What Every Child Should Know Along the Way* by Gail Martin. When Gary and I first read her manuscript, we were immediately impressed by its sensible and practical approach to teaching spiritual and life skills to children.

When we were raising our daughters Amy and Jennifer, we would have greatly appreciated having Gail's book as a reference to help us direct their character development and skills training. Your family is fortunate to have this tool.

As you carefully go through the workbook, you may realize that you may not have mastered some of the character and life skills presented. Ask the Lord to begin making the changes needed in your own life before you attempt training your children. As you will see, that includes not only practical, day-to-day skills, but character traits as well. Your effort to train your children in godly living must first begin *within your own heart* if you are to effectively transmit biblical values to them. They need to see you not only teaching those values, but also *living* them.

Pray as well that the Lord will give you the discernment to see which skills are appropriate for the age levels of each of your children. As they master one skill, do not be afraid to challenge them to the next level. Many of these teaching times will require patience, but God can provide whatever emotional resources you need to accomplish the task ahead.

In reading *What Every Child Should Know Along the Way*, please note how Gail carefully presents a principle to be learned and then demonstrates how that principle can be lived out in a practical manner. Also observe that the lists of skills are presented as *suggestions*, not as dogmatic rules to be taught in a legalistic manner. Remember: *context* is the key in all of your teachings. Do not let rigidity creep into your skills teaching. These lists are only given to provoke your thinking and to challenge you to do the best job you can in preparing your children for life.

When you are working through the *Practical Living Skills* section of this workbook, you may find it helpful to join together with other like-minded families. By doing so, you and your children can more effectively master the skills presented. By working together with other families, you can show your children what a blessing it can be to use their gifts and talents to help others in the body of Christ.

What Every Child Should Know Along the Way is a resource you will want to have within easy reach and review periodically to see how everyone in the family is growing in both character and skills.

We at Growing Families International are pleased to publish this book, and pray that it will help you prepare your children for life.

Ann Marie Ezzo
Growing Families International

Introduction

It is one of life's most precious moments when parents bring their new baby home from the hospital. Nothing can erase or replace that memory. The hours and days go by and, though tired from sleepless nights, the new parents' hearts thrill and wonder as they sacrificially care for their little baby. Nurturing, watching out for health and safety and meeting every need, all become a natural outflow of parenthood. The tiny infant is totally dependent, and the parents willingly provide the love and care he needs. But this season of dependence is short, and it does not take long before it is time to encourage the child to become more and more independent. Parents inevitably need to look ahead to the time when they will let go of their adult child. When the time comes, the child must be ready.

There are many skills and abilities that need to be taught to children before they venture out on their own. There are homemaking skills, academic skills, and interpersonal relationship skills, just to name a few. Schools, Sunday School classes, Scouting, 4-H clubs, and the like, all present opportunities for learning, but it cannot be assumed that these will teach your children all that they will need to know. The fact is, the *home* is the primary place for teaching children their skills for living, and parents are the most important teachers that they will ever have. Is teaching and training children easy? Not always. Nevertheless this training process must take place, for children must be taught. Therefore, it is important to accept this God-given responsibility, to begin, and then to press onward. God's Word says in Isaiah 40:11:

He tends His flock like a shepherd: He gathers the lambs in His arms and carries them close to his heart; He gently leads those that have young.

God tenderly loves our children and He has not left *us* alone in the task of raising them. He is gently leading us, moment by moment, day by day. Only as we follow the Shepherd's leading, and only as we look to Him for wisdom and strength, can we do this task He has called us to do.

Where is the parent is to begin? The starting place is with the attitude of the heart. However, it is not with the hearts of children, but rather, in the hearts of the parents. How parents perceive their children will determine how their children are trained. The Bible tells us in Psalms 127:3-5a:

Sons are a heritage from the Lord, children a reward from Him. Like arrows in the hands of a warrior are sons born in one's youth. Blessed is the man whose quiver is full of them.

Your children, whether through birth or adoption, are gifts from the hand of Almighty God. He has given them to you as a *reward* and a *blessing*. This gift that God has given to you is the most marvelous gift you will ever receive. And it carries with it the greatest, most awesome responsibility to which you will ever be entrusted.

When you look at your children, pause and stand in awe that you have been entrusted with these little lives. Embrace them with your arms, your time and your attention, and relish these fleeting years. Seek God's strength to love them. Love them enough to be gentle and tender. Love them enough to diligently train them and discipline them. Give them firm boundaries and clear expectations so they will thrive.

Instill in your children a firm foundation upon which they will build their entire lives. Uphold their dignity and speak kindly of them before others. Acknowledge that no one else was chosen to parent these children. God chose you.

AIM THEM STRAIGHT

Psalm 127:4: "Like arrows in the hands of a warrior..."

In Psalm 127 an analogy is drawn by the psalmist. He compares a warrior to a father and an arrow to his child. This warrior is a mighty man who spends time practicing his craft as an archer. He has studied his target. He knows it well. His arrows are straight and sharp. The irregularities in the arrow shaft are whittled and sanded smooth to provide for a clean and true flight. He aims, pulls his bowstring and releases his arrow accurately at the mark.

Likewise, the parent must know where he is aiming his children. He must be well acquainted with the target, which is the will of God as revealed in His Word. He must prepare his arrows (children) lovingly, correcting their rough places, sharpening them, and training them in righteousness. He must not shoot aimlessly, carelessly or ignorantly. He must take his time and aim them straight.

Consider the following "rules" developed by the Houston (Texas) Police Department. Reflect on what could become of arrows casually shot into space and allowed to haphazardly fall where they may. Remember: "If you fail to aim, you aim to fail."

Twelve rules for Raising Delinquent Children

1. Begin with infancy to give the child everything he wants. In this way he will grow up to believe the world owes him a living.

2. When he picks up bad words, laugh at him. This will make him think he's cute. It will also encourage him to pick up "cuter" phrases that will blow off the top of your head later.

3. Never give him any spiritual training. Wait till he is 21 and then let him "decide for himself."

4. Avoid use of the word "wrong." It may develop a guilt complex. This will condition him to believe that society is against him and he is being persecuted.

5. Pick up everything he leaves lying around (books, shoes, and clothing). Do everything for him so he will be experienced in throwing all responsibility on to others.

6. Let him read any printed matter he can get his hands on. Be careful that the silverware and drinking glasses are sterilized, but let his mind feast on garbage.

7. Quarrel frequently in the presence of your child. In this way he will not be too shocked when the home is broken up later.

8. Give a child all the spending money he wants. Never let him earn his own. Why should he have things as tough as *you* had them?

9. Satisfy his every craving for food, drink and comfort. See that every sensual desire is gratified. Denial of his desires may lead to harmful frustration.

10. Take his part against neighbors, teachers, and policemen. They are all prejudiced against your child.

11. When he gets into real trouble, apologize for yourself by saying, "I never could do anything with him."

12. Prepare for a life of grief.

In contrast to the haphazard arrow that misses the mark, God's Word defines for us the target for which we aim and the importance of being diligent to sharpen our arrows and prepare them for flight.

The teaching of the wise is a fountain of life, turning a man from the snares of death. Proverbs 13:14

Train up a child in the way he should go, and when he is old he will not turn from it. Proverbs 22:6

Discipline your son, and he will give you peace; he will bring delight to your soul. Proverbs 29:17

HOW TO USE THIS BOOK
This book is divided into the following categories:

> **Dynamic Devotional Living**
> **Cultivating Family Unity**
> **Gifts and Talents**
> **Biblical Character Traits**
> **Manners**
> **Practical Living Skills**
> **Personal Safety**

Please look over these categories and become familiar with the different set of skills each one offers. They can be used separately or concurrently since they deal with different areas of your children's lives. Many of the skills can be presented as the situation arises, others must be purposefully presented. They can be introduced by verbal instruction, role-playing or side by side "apprenticeship." It is my hope that these lists will become a source of enjoyable activities for your family to pursue together, and to give you a sense of direction as you prepare your children for adulthood.

The following pages consist of two primary aspects of child training: the spiritual and the practical. The spiritual includes the development of a devotional life, a proper perspective of self and the development of godly character. The practical skills required in daily life are built upon this spiritual framework. These skills in turn become the vehicles and opportunities through which the faith of your children is expressed to those around them. Therefore, if the foundation is well built (the priorities of the heart are right and the child views life and its various challenges through a godly, biblical perspective), then the ups and downs of life, and all the "dailiness" of living, have meaning and purpose.

If you employ this handbook when your children are little, start at the beginning and realize that these skills will take many years to instill. *Do not try to teach them everything all at once.* If your children are much older, you may find that there is much you can check off as already learned. There may also be some things to go back to reinforce. Even if your children are almost ready to leave home and you see much work to do, don't be discouraged. Choose a starting point as a family and proceed with the amount of time you have left. The worst thing you can do is throw your hands up in defeat and give up all together.

I would recommend that you use goal incentives such as charts, goal sheets, and achievement awards as you teach your children skills. These give children something to look forward to while reinforcing their progress in the right direction. They motivate, add a great deal of enthusiasm, and are just plain fun. There are many types of incentive charts available on the market today that you can utilize. You can also come up with your own. Make racetracks and race to the finish line. Make a thermometer and climb up the degrees, or buy some gold stars and accumulate an agreed upon number of stars to earn a special reward or privilege. Use your creativity. Keep in mind, however, that no one chart will last indefinitely. Once the new skill is understood and fully attained, then it should become a natural part of their lives. And, since new skills to be learned are just over the horizon, the fun and enthusiasm can be continued. Just remember, the goal is not to focus on charts, but to teach your children the necessary skills that they will use for a lifetime.

Children:
Multifaceted jewels
Fashioned by God's Hand.
A priceless treasure,
A source of joy.

Chapter One

Dynamic Devotional Living

⚜

What is "Dynamic Devotional Living?" These words, as defined in *Webster's Encyclopedic Unabridged Dictionary of the English Language*, are as follows:

Dynamic – *adj.* 1. pertaining to or characterized by energy or effective action; vigorously active or forceful; energetic; 2. of or pertaining to force or power; of or pertaining to force related to motion.

Devotion – *noun* 1. profound dedication; consecration; 2. the ready will to perform that which belongs to the service of God.

Live – *verb* 1. to pass life in a specified manner; 2. to direct or regulate one's life.

To sum it up, Dynamic Devotional Living is...

> *... being vigorously active and profoundly dedicated*
> *to the love, praise and service of God;*
> *resulting in the power of God*
> *affecting further life transformation,*
> *thereby producing the joy of holy,*
> *Christ-like living.*

It may sound like a mouth-full, but it communicates the essence of the Christian life. Christians are to live to the full measure of their God-given abilities – moment by moment acknowledging His presence and giving glory and praise to God for His love, forgiveness, provision, protection, salvation and more. Continuing in this manner, believers are able to see God's dynamic power affecting life changes that bring them into conformity with His son, Jesus Christ (Rom. 8:29). Living such lives, as well as leading our children into this manner of living is the challenging, yet compelling task before us all.

Dynamic Devotional Living comes directly out of Deuteronomy 6: 4-9:

Hear O Israel: The Lord our God, the Lord is one. Love the Lord your God with all your heart and with all your soul and with all your strength. These commandments that I give you today are to be upon your hearts. Impress them on your children. Talk about them when you sit at home and when you walk along the road, when you lie down and when you get up. Tie them as symbols on your hands and bind them on your foreheads. Write them on the door frames of your houses and on your gates.

Dynamic Devotional Living then, becomes the natural outflow of a life completely committed to living for the Lord and pleasing Him in all respects. This single-focused intent of loving God and seeking to please Him in response to His love for us, is the foundational framework upon which all areas of life are built. The purpose for every moral, intellectual and practical skill that your children will ever learn will pivot on this vertex. Hence, how a child grows in the spiritual realm will determine their view of the world, their character development and every aspect of their behavior.

It is no wonder then, that God has given parents such a specific and important commandment regarding children. His command is that parents are to faithfully impress God's Word on their children's hearts in everything they do; always incorporating the knowledge of His presence in every area of life. It is a lifelong process that is to be perpetuated from one generation to the next – continually passing on the truth of God's Word regarding the love and character of God as well as His plan for the lives of His children. It should be as natural to speak about the Lord as it is to "sit at home, walk along the road, lie down or get up." Take time to read Deuteronomy 10:12-11:32. In this passage God makes His desire clear as to how important it is that parents live in reverence to God before their children and faithfully teach them all His ways. As your children see you model a personal devotional life and maintain a family devotional life they will learn how to have their own personal devotions, how to grow in their own personal relationship with the Lord, and ultimately understand how to pass on this knowledge to their own children.

UNSTRUCTURED DEVOTIONS

Devotional living occurs in many ways. Sometimes it is structured, such as during family devotions or in corporate worship. Much of the time it is unstructured and takes place in the simple everyday conversations and activities of life. These are the "sit at home, walk along the road, lie down or get up" devotions spoken of in Deuteronomy chapter 6.

Natural conversations are a form of unstructured devotions. They can be initiated through your circumstances or your surroundings. For instance, the following situations or surroundings could spark these topics of conversation:

LOOKING AT PLANTS:
God's creation
The parable of the sower
God's gift of rain
God's gift of food

LOOKING AT ANIMALS:
God's variation in creation
Noah's ark
The Passover Lamb
Our responsibility to care for animals with kindness

DOING THE LAUNDRY:
How our hearts were once dirty, but are now washed clean
Serving and helping one another
Being a diligent and cheerful worker

GOING TO THE GROCERY STORE:
God is our provider
God provides food for our bodies
God provides food for our hearts through His Word
Our bodies are the temple of the Holy Spirit and we need to take care of them

SEEING A NEW BABY:
God knew the little baby before he was born
God is the creator of all life
Jesus came to die for even this little one

The list can go on and on. The goal of these natural conversations is for children to see the mighty hand of God in everything they do, to observe and experience, and to acknowledge His presence wherever they are.

One opportunity that can come from these natural conversations is to talk of the love of God and His wonderful gift of salvation. In leading a child (or anyone) to Christ, there are some basic facts that need to be taught.

Truths to Teach About Salvation:

- **Who God is:** The divine attributes of God transcend all that we can know. God is completely other than we are. He is without beginning or end, He is everywhere present, all powerful, unchanging, completely sovereign in rule and majesty, perfectly holy and righteous, all wise, all knowing, all goodness, truth, mercy, justice, and love. God is the creator of all that exists, and all that exists is for His glory. (Gen.1:1; Psalms 100:3; Heb. 11:3; Rev. 4:11; Psalms 19:1)

- **Who man is:** God wondrously created man and woman in His own image. Yet, though we are created in God's image, we do not have the infinite extent of His attributes. God is wholly sufficient; we are not. We were made to depend upon God, not ourselves, to meet all our needs. God also designed a plan for each of our lives that was determined by His goodness and wisdom. The resulting purpose and delight of men and women as we live each day is to personally know God, as He has revealed Himself through the Bible, to worship and glorify Him, and to enjoy Him now and forever. (Gen. 1:26-27, 31; 1 Cor. 10:31; Psalms 73:25-26; Eph. 2:10)

- **What sin is:** The first man and woman were created without sin and were in perfect fellowship with God. However, they chose to disobey and sin against God. We follow in their footsteps. Sin is any attitude or action that falls short of God's standard or Law; it is any disobedience to Him in thought, word or deed. The Bible rightly concludes that "All have sinned and fall short of the glory of God." (Rom. 3:23) Our sin results in serious consequences. Because God is perfectly holy, He cannot dwell alongside our sin. Because sin is a violation against the holiness of God, it carries with it a penalty. The penalty for sin is death and separation from God forever in hell – a place of eternal darkness, weeping and torment. Sin leaves us eternally lost, desperately needing to be saved. (Rom. 5:12; James 4:17; Rom. 3:23; Rom. 6:23)

- **God's gift of salvation:** Even though we rightly deserve death and separation from God, He extends to us a gift. That gift is eternal life and a restored fellowship with Him, through His Son, Jesus Christ. God loved the world so much that He sent His Son to take our penalty of death upon Himself. Jesus, who is fully God, also became fully man for our sakes and lived among us. He experienced all that we experience and identified with all our weaknesses, yet He is without sin. Because Jesus is fully God, He too, is perfectly holy. In spite of our sinfulness, He showed immeasurable and unconditional love toward us by taking upon Himself the deserved punishment of all mankind. He bore our every sin upon the cross when He suffered and died in our place, saving each of us from the penalty we owed. After three days in the grave He arose alive and appeared to many people. He then returned to heaven where He is preparing a place for those who believe in Him and have personally placed their trust in Him as their Savior and Lord. Because He still lives, we too can know that we shall one day live in heaven with Him. (John 3:16; Phil. 2:6-7; Acts 4:12; Rom. 5:8; 1 John 2:2; 2 Cor. 5:21; 1 Peter 3:18; John 14:1-7; 1 Cor. 15:3-8)

- **Receiving God's gift:** Salvation cannot be earned. It is a gift. Like other gifts, it is offered in love and must be taken from the giver's hand and accepted before it becomes one's own. Salvation is a gift that the receiver must not only desire, but also must recognize how desperately it is needed. Each of us must acknowledge that we have sinned and that there is no way that we can pay the penalty for our own sin and restore our relationship with God. Only then are we able to accept by faith what Jesus accomplished for us when He died for our every sin upon the cross. Because of the love of Christ and His death in our place, God forgives us of all our sin: past, present, and future. In place of our sin, God gives us the perfect righteousness of Jesus. This wonderful gift marvelously restores us into a right relationship with God and we can look forward to eternal life in God's glorious presence. (John 1:12; Rom. 10:9; 1 Cor. 5:17; Eph. 2:8-9; Titus 3:3-7; 1 John 2:2)

- **Growing as a Christian:** When we individually receive God's gift of salvation, trusting in what Christ has done on our behalf and committing our life to Him, we become a child of God. As one of His children, He wants us to grow in faith. Faith grows as we read the Bible, pray, worship and fellowship with other believers. To help us in this growth God has given us another gift

– The Holy Spirit. The Spirit comes and lives within the hearts of believers, leading them and empowering them to become more like Christ and fulfilling the purpose and plan that God has for their lives. Believers who love God will want to turn away from the old sinful ways of the past and live in joyful obedience to the Word of God, seeking to please Him and glorify Him in all they do. (1 John 1:9; 1 John 3:21-24; 1 John 5:11-13; 1 John 2:5-6; Eph. 4:30; Mark 12:28-31; Col 1:10-14; 3:1-17; 2 John 6)

• **Prayer of Commitment:** If you or your child desire to receive this free gift of salvation, consider praying the following prayer:

Dear Heavenly Father, I recognize that I am a sinner and that my sin deserves punishment and separation from Your presence. I accept what Jesus has done in my place when He died on the cross for my sin, freeing me from the penalty I owe. Thank you for forgiving me of all my sins and for your gift of eternal life. I receive Jesus Christ as my Savior and Lord of my life. Thank you for your Holy Spirit that will teach me how to turn away from my old sinful ways and follow in joyful obedience after you. I gratefully commit my life to you. In Jesus Name, I pray, Amen.

The word "salvation" is an all-inclusive word of the gospel. It brings together all the redemptive acts and processes: Justification, redemption, grace, propitiation, imputation, forgiveness, sanctification, and glorification. These marvelous truths, along with the importance of baptism, celebration of the Lord's Supper and the anticipation and preparation for Christ's return can be further explored in your devotional time with your children.

Salvation is a personal experience; it cannot be obtained by parents on behalf of their children. Each person must receive this gift individually. Many children raised in Christian communities have a clear knowledge of who God is but may not know Him personally. They can know all the right answers, and yet never put their trust in Jesus Christ and accept His sacrifice made on their behalf.

Pray that God will give you the great privilege of leading your children to a personal relationship with their Savior and Lord, Jesus Christ.

STRUCTURED DEVOTIONS

Family devotions or family worship are a form of structured devotions. These are times that are specifically set aside for a formal reading and discussion of God's Word, prayer and other aspects of worship. Though these activities take place at church, they are not to stop there. They must also be happening within the family at home. Though starting and consistently maintaining family devotions can be challenging and takes thought and planning, the blessings far outweigh the effort. You may want to consider the following as you plan for your family devotions.

Why Have Family Devotions?

Family devotions provide an opportunity to teach your children about their Father in heaven who loves them with an everlasting love. It is here that they can learn about their Savior and His love and sacrifice for them. Bible stories can be introduced that tell about people, their obedience or disobedience to God and the resulting consequences (good or bad) of their actions.

In addition, family devotions present an opportunity to set before your children the biblical standard of living. During this time you can teach them what is the right behavior in various circumstances *before* the need arises, not after the children are already in trouble! Never assume that your children have learned correct behaviors unless *you* have taught them! After the right biblical principles have been taught you will then have a reference point to refer back to when behavioral issues arise.

Keep in mind that you have been entrusted with these little lives for a season – a very short season. When the time of their childhood comes closer to an end, you will want to be working on transferring your children from obedience to you as parents, to obedience based solely upon their devotion to God. See that your children are equipped to seek God's will for themselves when you are no longer in the picture. How can you do that? By continually pointing them to God's Word as the sole authority for their lives and teaching them as much as you can of what it says. This is followed by encouraging them and training them to spend time reading the Bible on their own; teaching them to listen as God speaks to them through His Word as they grow in their own personal relationship with the living God.

Psalms 119:11: Thy word have I hid in my heart, that I may not sin against thee.

Set Up a Time for Family Devotions

The time for family devotions can be morning, noon or night. Once you have set a time, make it a regular part of your routine. The frequency can depend on your family schedule as well. For some it will be every day. For others it may be three times a week. Even doing it once a week is a wonderful place to begin.

Set Up a Location

You can meet in the same place or change it from time to time. Everyone likes the feeling of refreshment that an occasional change can bring. You may want to begin around the kitchen table, in the family room, living room, etc. The choice is yours.

Consider the Ages of Your Children When Choosing Material

There are many different resources available to families today, and they appeal to a variety of age groups. If you have very young children, you will probably want to begin with the simpler and shorter stories at first. Consider looking at material from a child's eye view. Your children will always appreciate and enjoy books with beautiful illustrations. You will find your non-readers picking up well-illustrated books and slowly looking at the pictures, recalling in their minds the stories that you have already read to them. What a beautiful way to instill a love for God's Word!

As your children get older you can begin to equip them to become Bible scholars in their own right. Provide more in-depth resources (such as Bible atlases) that illustrate what the Bible lands were like in the past and what they are like today. Teach them how to use a concordance, a commentary and a Bible dictionary. Give them devotional and study materials that are age appropriate and that can give them direction in their studies.

Encourage your older children to set aside a regular time for their own personal devotions. Suggest that they keep a journal to record the spiritual lessons they learn from God's Word and from their daily experiences (a priceless treasure they will cherish all their days). What a joy it is when you see your children meeting with God, fully equipped to study God's Word and apply it to their own lives.

Make Family Devotions an Enjoyable Time

Create an atmosphere that is delightful, and where fun can abide along with the serious importance of God's Word. What can be done to make devotions an enjoyable experience? Consider the following suggestions:

- Use beautifully illustrated Bible storybooks for the youngest eyes (or the oldest) to enjoy. Let them see the pictures while you read the stories. Ask simple questions to see if they understand what you are reading.

- Draw along with the story. Give each child a piece of paper or a tablet and have them illustrate the story with stick figures as you read. Then let each of them share and explain what they drew.

- Parents may be the first readers who lead in family devotions. As your family grows, the privilege of reading can be passed around, with everyone following along in their own Bibles.

- Parents can ask discussion questions such as:
  1. What is the principle of this story?
  2. What did the people do that was right or wrong?
  3. Does it apply to us today? How?
  4. What actions does this new knowledge require of me? Confession? Forgiveness? Obedience? Thanksgiving?
  5. Can I share this with someone else?

- Quiz each other on what was read. Read the passage for the day and then go around and have each person ask another person a question. That way you can ensure that they are listening. Not only do they have to come up with an intelligent question but they have to answer one as well! (You can even try to stump each other by trying to remember specific details such as the number of cubits in the height of the ark or the weight of Goliath's spearhead.)

- Act out a Bible story! Select a portion of Scripture that lends itself to family members playing different parts. The story of Christ's birth is one such passage. Reenacting this portion of Scripture can also become a meaningful Christmas tradition.

- Memorize scripture together as a family. Verses can be chosen from Sunday school, Bible clubs, Christian or home school, or from the passages that you read as a family. There are many different children's songs that can help in memorizing scripture. Using simple illustrations on paper or using sign language can also help to "hide God's Word in their heart."

Sing Together

Music can be an enriching part of your family devotions. Incorporate choruses and introduce the hymns of the faith. You can even make up your own songs! Sing *a cappella,* put on a tape or CD, or have your budding instrumentalist accompany the family. Take time to read through the words to traditional hymns. They are filled with wonderful doctrine as well as inspirational expressions of love and faith toward God and His continual faithfulness toward us. Reading through hymns and discussing what they mean will greatly enhance their worship alone, as a family and at church.

Let your family be one that enjoys singing together and praising God in worship. This can happen not only during family devotions, but also while doing chores together, or driving in the car. You don't have to have beautiful voices and always be right on key. God said to "make a joyful noise," remember? So sing!

Pray Together

Prayer often occurs at meals, during devotions and at bedtime, but it doesn't need to stop there. Teach and model for your children that anytime during the day or night they can stop and speak to the Lord. Prayer can take place while doing homework, home schooling, chores, in response to a need expressed over the phone, in the car, after an injury, during an illness, etc. Prayer should become as natural as breathing. As the apostle Paul wrote, "Pray without ceasing." (I Thessalonians 5:17)

TEACH YOUR CHILDREN HOW TO PRAY:

- Teach your children how to pray intelligently. Do not simply let them repeat memorized prayers, or get in the habit of saying the same things every time.

- Teach them that they can talk to God (whom they cannot see) in the same way they talk to someone they can see. Help them realize that God listens, delights in, and answers their prayers.

- Teach them that God answers prayer in many ways. Sometimes He says, "No." Sometimes He says, "Later." And sometimes He says, "Yes!" either in the manner that was asked or in a manner that they would never have been imagined!

- Share requests that are appropriate for their ages. These can be personal needs from within the family or from friends. Prayer needs can come from the church, community or world. (You can also teach them the difference between "sharing prayer requests" and "gossip.")

- Keep a family prayer list, so they can see how God answers prayer. (See Family Prayer Journal on page 25.)

- Teach them the Lord's Prayer (Matthew 6:9-13) and talk about what it means.

- Give them instruction in the many elements included in prayer using a method such the acronym ACTS:

  Adoration – Praising God for who He is.

  Confession – Agreeing with God in regard to your personal sin.

  Thanksgiving – Thanking Him for His forgiveness, provision and blessing.

  Supplication – Bringing before Him your needs as well as the needs of others.

Many aspects of family devotions may feel awkward and uncomfortable at first, especially if you did not grow up with this as a part of your childhood experience. However, if you begin when your children are young, it will become a customary part of their lives and they will anticipate and enjoy this family time. If this will be a new experience incorporated into your family and your children are older, you may sense some resistance to the change of routine; however the more you do it, the easier and more natural it will become. You may also become aware of the unseen spiritual war. The last thing Satan wants is for families to be united around God's Word. Satan is opposed to Christian homes impacting this world for Christ and to the next generation having a spirit-empowered, personal walk with the Lord. However, that is God's plan for us. Therefore, stand firm against the fiery darts of the enemy. Persevere and God will strengthen you.

God has commanded His children to pass on the knowledge of Himself from one generation to another. What a serious responsibility. What a grand privilege!

God's Word:
Foundation for our lives.
Teaching, correcting,
encouraging, equipping;
impacting our families,
our communities,
our world.

FAMILY PRAYER JOURNAL

Now to Him who is able to do immeasurably more than all we ask or imagine, according to His power that is at work within us, to Him be glory in the church and in Christ Jesus throughout all generations, forever and ever! Amen! Ephesians 3:20-21

Date	Request	Date	Answer

Chapter Two

Cultivating
Family Unity

After a child is born, new parents greet each stage of their baby's development with great delight. The first time he smiles, coos, laughs, crawls, walks, and talks, are celebratory moments. Before you realize the passage of time, the infant has become a young child and is gleefully playing outside in the sunshine. Perhaps a second child joins the family and prayers are sent heavenward that the two will always play together peacefully and share happily. It does not take long, however, before reality strikes and it becomes clear that children, too, have a sin nature! Words such as, "Mine!" and "Mom, he's not being fair!" ring in the air. Note the following:

Toddler Property Laws
1. If I like it, it's mine.
2. If it's in my hand, it's mine.
3. If I can take it from you, it's mine.
4. If I had it a little while ago, it's mine.
5. If it's mine, it must never appear to be yours in any way.
6. If I'm doing or building something, all the pieces are mine.
7. If it looks just like mine, it's mine.
   (Author Unknown)

Is this funny? Yes, it is funny to read. But, it is not so funny when you have to deal with it. After all, scenarios such as these can arise with siblings of every age, not just with toddlers! Parents realize they often need the wisdom of Solomon to solve the squabbles of their precious children.

Sibling conflict is normal. Loving and respectful interaction with others does not come naturally (selfishness, however, does). Children need to learn *how* to love and get along with brothers and sisters (as well as with others outside the family).

Happily, the most opportune place to teach these skills is within the Christian home. The home is the classroom and laboratory, the Bible is the textbook, and the parents are the teachers. Patient and consistent modeling by the teachers is essential in order to effectively instruct the students how to love others. If harsh criticism, rejection, and impatience are portrayed, than that is what the student will learn. If, on the other hand, words of encouragement, acceptance, gentleness and patience are offered then these will be the traits acquired. Never forget that far more is "caught" by example than can *ever* be "taught" by words. Building family unity is not a one-semester course. Rather it is a course that requires frequent instruction, repetition and ongoing practice, in order for a genuine spirit of unity to be attained.

Though it can be a challenge, teaching and training are essential to a strong family unit. Instill in your children the unique identity and interdependence of your family. God has given you to each other for a purpose. Encourage your children to value one another and appreciate how uniquely God has made each one. When brothers and sisters are best friends, the home will be blessed, and the world will notice.

The following quotation serves as an example of two brothers who were best friends and changed the course of world history. Their relationship will inspire you to cultivate the atmosphere in your own home where brothers and sisters look to each other – not as adversaries – but as indispensable friends with whom they share their joys, sorrows, dreams, defeats and victories.

Neither could have mastered the problem alone. As inseparable as twins, they are indispensable to each other.

Bishop Milton Wright

Father of Wilbur and Orville.

January 16, 1904

From the time we were little children my brother Orville and myself lived together, played together, worked together and, in fact, thought together. We usually owned all of our toys in common, talked over our thoughts and aspirations so that nearly everything that was done in our lives has been the result of conversations, sugges-tions and discussions between us.

Wilbur Wright, April 3, 1912

Quoted from *How We Made The First Flight* by Orville Wright.
U.S. Department of Transportation; Federal Aviation Administration

Who can deny the worldwide impact that these two brothers made as they discovered the secrets of aerodynamics? But first, these two had to discover the joy of cooperation, sharing, mutual encouragement and friendship.

The following sections offer ideas that can help in creating an environ-ment where your children can grow in mutual love and where the family cre-ates a strong sense of identity. Some of the suggestions include activities that you can do as a family. These provide the links that hold you together, as well as make important installments into their childhood memory banks. Other suggestions include the messages that you send to their hearts that teach them the right attitudes toward one another and that cultivate mutual love.

FAMILY TOGETHERNESS

Family activities are wonderful for drawing parents and siblings together. It not only unites the family during the planning, preparation and executing of the activity, but it also brings the family together for years to come. This hap-pens as each member looks back and remembers the events they all have shared. These shared activities will someday become your children's precious memories. And it is memories that become the reference points in time that will provide your children with a sense of what their fleeting childhood was like. When they look back, they will have little recollection of the routine aspects of life: three meals a day, clothes to wear, and chores being done. However, they *will* remember the family picnics at the beach, kite flying in the meadow, and the traditions at Christmas. Give your family memories.

It is a well-known saying that if you aim at nothing, you will hit it every time. So if you plan to do nothing, that is exactly what you will do! Therefore, if you do not set aside time for special activities with your family, you can be sure that every weekend will be busy with routine chores and you will won-der where the years have gone. So, take time to pause from the hectic daily schedule, and set aside a time to make plans. With your calendar in hand, sit at the table with a cup of tea or under a tree in the park and plan the next three to six months. Prior to your official planning session, ask your children to describe their favorite things to do and places to go. Incorporate these ideas into your planning. In addition, think further down the road – such as the next three to five years. What larger vacations can you possibly plan for? As your children get older, this planning can be done together as a family.

Here are some ideas for family activities. You can see that the list can go on and on:

- Zoo and park outings
- Hiking
- Camping
- BBQ's or picnics
- Biking
- Swimming
- Bowling
- Ice or roller-skating
- Visiting a shut-in
- Helping an elderly couple or a widow
- Visiting a museum
- Having "board game" night
- Pizza and movie night (either out or at home)
- Read a book night
- Decorating the house for a holiday
- Driving around and counting Christmas lights
- July 4th celebrations
- Doing a church/community work of service together
- Traveling by train to destinations near or far
- Visiting state or national historical sites
- Doing a short-term mission as a family

Plan on one family activity per month. You could plan for more, but it may be better to start small, rather then overwhelm yourselves. (It is fun to join with other families in an activity, but it is very important to make time to be just with your *own* family.)

Plan not only for activities that you can do as a family, but plan for one-on-one time as well. Set aside "date nights" with your children. Every other week or even once a month, Mom or Dad can rotate taking a child out on a "date." These dates can include going for a walk, fishing, bowling, shopping, dining at a fast food restaurant or even having a simple ice-cream cone together. Let the time be fun and filled with positive conversation. Get to know your children. See them for who they are as they gradually unfold into their adult lives. Use the time to reaffirm your love for them. Encourage them and tell them of the strengths you see in their character. Avoid using these times as a forum for telling your children their "problems." This is a time to *build* relationships! Dates do not have to be expensive, but the investment of time is of immeasurable value.

When your children are of driving age, send *them* out together for an occasional date night. (A pre-approved activity, of course!) Let it simply be a time for them to have fun and be together. Their teen years together are very short – so make them count!

Date nights are also an important part of a marriage. Mom and Dad, you *need* to go out. It is a valuable investment in your marriage to spend one-on-on time together. As the years go by, people grow and change and it is essential that you keep on growing in your love and understanding of one another. Date nights away from the normal routines provide you a chance to focus on one another, build shared interests together and reaffirm your love for each other. It cannot be overstated how vital it is for children to see that Mom and Dad are still very much in love. This greatly adds to their sense of security; for if there is strength and unity in the marriage, there will be strength and unity in the family. When the empty nest comes, and it will, there needs to remain a strong and loving marriage that will continue to flourish for many years to come.

Plan for "talk times." Set aside opportunities when you can just sit and talk. This can be done all together as a family or one-on-one with a child. One-on-one times can happen on a date, in a rocking chair or at a bedside as you tuck your child in for the night. It is times such as these that you may be given a peek into the rooms of your child's heart that are often kept hidden. These can be gentle and loving times that deepen and reaffirm your bonds of love; times when feelings or thoughts (not always so easily shared) can be spoken safely. When your children arrive at the teenage years, they can be very busy and it can be tough to find time just to talk and listen (emphasis on listen). Often it will be late in the evening, after their activities and schoolwork are done, that they will have a few minutes to unwind before they get into bed. These moments can provide the chance to get a glimpse into their private world – their visions for the future, new found friends, struggles with school or relationships, spiritual doubts and victories. It is tempting, as parents, to go to bed earlier than our teens after we have had a long day ourselves, but periodically stay up late, step into their rooms and visit. Bring up a couple bowls of ice cream or popcorn and listen, talk, and listen some more. You may be up for a while and lose a little sleep, but you will be glad you did.

Training your children takes time, planning takes time, activities take time, talking and listening takes time. Make that time a priority. This important investment of time is what facilitates the building of strong relationships. And it is this unique collection of relationships that creates your distinct family identity. When the sense of family identity is strong and a child feels loved and accepted, then they know who they are and where they belong. Time, love, acceptance, fun, laughter...what greater gifts could you possibly give your family?

SIBLINGS AS FRIENDS

Psalm 133:1: How good and pleasant it is when brothers live together in unity.

Cultivating mutual love between siblings is similar to the cultivating of soil for a garden. The heart's soil of your children must be prepared and tended to gently and faithfully. Soil that is properly tilled will allow the seeds of right behaviors and attitudes to go down deep, and produce a bountiful harvest. Tilling this soil requires that the weeds and stones be removed and cast away. The weeds of the heart are those behaviors that choke out love and sow disunity in the family. They can be disloyalty, dishonesty, discourtesy and disrespect. The stones are the hard and harsh behaviors thrown at one another that are hurtful and damaging. These include harsh criticism, belittling, insults and unkind teasing. Such weeds and stones need to continually be removed and desirable seeds sown in their place. Desirable seeds are the teaching and modeling of Christ-like attitudes and actions that you plant in their hearts. Among these seeds are found compassion, kindness, humility, gentleness, and acceptance toward one another; an acceptance that values one another's God given uniqueness. Love, encouragement, patience and prayers are the water and nourishment that cause these seeds to sprout and grow. The harvested fruits that are borne from this garden are a lifelong love, trust, unselfish dedication, and mutual support shared during the joys and the sorrows of life. Within the garden of the family the intimate knowledge of one another's individuality is respected, protected and cherished by each other.

Below are examples of different types of seeds that you can be planting in the hearts of your children.

- Remind and emphasize *verbally* that brothers and sisters are each other's best friends. When they are playing together well, praise and encourage them for treating each other as best friends should.

- When they fight, remind them that it is okay to disagree over something, but best friends try to work things out without getting angry or hurting each other. When they need to work something out, send them off to another room to talk until they have resolved it to their *mutual* satisfaction. This will require parental involvement in the beginning to help them learn this skill, and to insure that the older child does not simply intimidate the younger sibling. Encourage them to hug or shake hands when the conflict is resolved.

- Encourage your children to verbally praise one another. Help them look for opportunities to build one another up with encouraging words.

- If a sibling slips and says something unkind to a brother or sister, have them apologize and then say one or two nice things that they appreciate about the other person. Perhaps such an unkindness could also be amended by an act of loving service. For instance, the offender can make the bed of the offended for the next few days or do one of their chores.

- Teach your children to share. It is acceptable for a child to have extra special or fragile treasures that are kept private, however, the majority of what a child possesses can be shared. (It helps to remind them that God owns all things and He has asked them to be His unselfish stewards.)

- Encourage them to be sensitive to the needs of each other. When a brother or sister seems sad or discouraged, teach them how to come alongside, listen and express compassion. Point out ways that they can lovingly serve each other, perhaps even volunteering to do a chore for someone who is ill or struggling. These acts of love may not come naturally, so they must be taught.

- Teach your children to rejoice for one another when something good happens (a birthday, a special award, etc.) instead of feeling jealous. Help them realize that on another day they will be the one with the special honor.

- When playing games, teach them to play fair, be happy for the winner, be gracious to the one who did not win, and be ready to shake hands at the end of the game.

- Let siblings share a room together (if they are of the same gender). Have them mutually participate in the decorating *and* cleaning. Teach them to have respect for each other's treasured possessions. This helps them learn to cooperate and to show preference to one another.

- If siblings do share a room, allow them a few minutes of "talk time" together at night after they are in bed. This provides a great opportunity for their relationship to deepen and grow.

- Encourage the common interests that they share. For instance, if it is music, suggest that they sing or play instrumental duets together. If it is sports, help them to find an opportunity to play together on a team; if a hobby, equip them with space to work together.

- Giving presents at Christmas and at birthdays provides a great opportunity to promote the value of giving to others. Help provide jobs where they can earn money for gifts or purchase supplies with which to make their own gifts. Teach them to thoughtfully plan their gifts, considering the personality and preferences of the one who will be the recipient.

- Be careful not to allow friends over so much that they supersede family times.

- Remind your children that when they are older, they may not have the same friends that they now enjoy because people move away and circumstances change. However, they will always have each other.

- Teach your children how to turn to each other with personal needs so that they can be supporting and praying for each other.

- Occasionally, go around the dinner table and have *all* family members share what they really enjoy about one another. This can be a lovely tradition to include around the Thanksgiving holiday table.

- Look for opportunities to unify the family in simple ways. Make it a habit to frequently use words such as, "I love you," "I am so proud of you," and "I feel blessed to be your mom/dad." Remember the commercial that says, "Reach out and touch someone...?" Sometimes we forget just how important that can be. Love can wonderfully be communicated by a light squeeze when you walk by, a ruffle of the hair, the holding of a little hand, an arm around the shoulder, clasping hands around the table during prayer, and the delightful and hilarious crush of a great big "family hug."

- Parents: When your children grow into teenagers they will quickly become as tall or taller than you are. Soon you will realize that you have a household full of adults and there are no more little ones around. You will remember the days when they were little, and how easy it was to pick them up, hold them on your lap, kiss them on the cheek or snuggle up closely. Just don't forget that even though your teenagers have grown into adult bodies and are going through many changes, they are still your children. They still need your hugs, an arm around the shoulder, an occasional kiss on the check, and a tuck into bed. Reach out to them and keep on reaching out. They still need you!

The family is not something to be worshipped or idolized, but rather to be cherished and treated as the precious gift that it is. The family has been designed by God as the place for nurturing, for training, and for the expressing of unconditional love between parents and children. This is the beautiful picture which points each generation to the love of the heavenly Father. Friends and loved ones outside of the family will always be a very important part of our lives. The church is, in many ways, an extension of our families, and is in fact, our *eternal* family. But, before we can effectively reach out and care for others, we must first learn to lovingly minister to the people whom God has especially gifted us: our family.

May the Lord bless and strengthen you
as you build a Christian home,
where mutual respect,
kindness, love
and laughter abound.

Chapter Three

Gifts and Talents

T here is a tremendous amount of information currently available about developing your child's self-esteem. In addition, much has been written about how important it is to recognize and encourage a child's natural gifts and talents. As parents, are we to strive to develop self-esteem in our children? Should we encourage their gifts and talents? The answer to the second question is simple: Yes, we should encourage their spiritual and natural gifts and talents as a way of bringing glory to God through their lives.

The answer to the first question, however, is more complex. The modern-day self-esteem movement tells parents that children are "at risk" if they have a low self-esteem. To avoid this "danger" children need to be encouraged to "believe" in themselves and in their inherent goodness. This philosophy has even infiltrated the church and teaches that a person must love himself before he can love God or others.

But it should *never* be your goal to teach your children to feel "good" about themselves. Your goal should be to teach them to feel "right" about themselves when they are obeying God and living according to His moral law. Feeling "right" about their behavior is the by-product of two things: humility before God and obedience to God.

A child who is taught to humbly obey God will feel "right" about himself because his worth is based on God's loving acceptance and approval of him. There is nothing a child can perform or produce that will ever change His love. God wholly accepts and unconditionally loves. In response to who He is and because of what He has done, the child of God humbly worships, and obediently lives for the One who alone is worthy of our highest esteem.

Feeling "right" about oneself also involves accepting the life circumstances in which God has placed him. Psalm 139:13-16, speaks of God's sovereign hand in the creation of each of His children:

For you created my inmost being; you knit me together in my mother's womb. I praise you because I am fearfully and wonderfully made; your works are wonderful, I know that full well. My frame was not hidden from you when I was made in the secret place. When I was woven together in the depths of the earth, your eyes saw my unformed body. All the days ordained for me were written in your book before one of them came to be.

Each person, young and old alike, must acknowledge that every aspect of what makes them who they are has been ordained by the loving hand of God for His purposes and His glory. There is no facet of our being that comes as a surprise to Him. He is the potter. We are the clay. As the clay, there are certain unchangeables that that we must graciously embrace in order to accept how God has made us. These unchangeable are:

- Where in this world and when in history you were born
- Parents
- Siblings
- Birth order
- Gender
- Physical features
- Abilities and weaknesses
- Race/Nationality
- Growing old
- When you die

Parents and children alike need to teach their hearts to accept these unchangeables and say:

"Thank you, Lord, that you have made me just the way I am. Thank you, that I don't have to be compared to others or try to measure up to any standard in order for you to love me. Thank you, God, that you love me just the same in victory or defeat. Thank you, that I don't need to struggle to find self-worth, because true worth comes from being in Christ. Thank you, that I can freely reach out to others because in you I feel loved and secure. Thank you, that in all my weaknesses you are strong. Thank you, that I can offer up every area of my life to you. Thank you, that for every day you have ordained for me on this earth I have the honor of bringing you glory."

ACKNOWLEDGING GIFTS AND TALENTS

When we find our worth in Christ alone, does this mean we should ignore our natural gifts and talents, or neglect developing skills that would enhance our lives and better equip us in our service to God and others? No. Though gifts, talents and skills are not the basis for our worth, God has placed them in our lives for a purpose.

So, what do you do with natural talents? What about the spiritual gifts that the Holy Spirit bestows on all believers in Christ? First of all, identify what they are. Secondly go to the "Source" with thankfulness. People *have* nothing and *are* nothing aside from what God has put into their being. Help your child recognize that God has a special hand on their lives and He has gifted them in a unique way. Encourage them to find out just what their spiritual gifts and natural talents are. Teach them to thank God for His special design and for the gifts and talents that He has given. Guide them so they will be prepared to use them for the Lord.

These talents and gifts can be in the following areas (but are not limited to):

TALENTS
Music – Singing Or Instrumental
Athletics
Art
Drama
Speaking
Writing
Mechanics
Mathematics
Engineering
Manual Dexterity
Physical Strength
Science
Sewing
Cooking
Carpentry
Computer Aptitude
Many other talents

SPIRITUAL GIFTS
Wisdom
Knowledge
Discernment
Pastoring
Teaching
Administration
Helps
Exhortation
Mercy
Giving
Faith
Hope
Love
Prayer
Hospitality
Other gifts used to build up the body of Christ

Once your children have discovered their God-given gifts and talents, help them to develop them. Guide them, direct them, and give them opportunities to grow. Teach them to be good stewards of their gifts in the same way they are to be stewards of all the other areas of their lives. Help them to view their gift as a platform from which they can share their faith, serve others and glorify God.

It is exciting to know that each person is gifted in a different way. Therefore, comparing one person against another is totally unnecessary. God has not made all His children alike. Some are born with many natural abilities. Some are born with seemingly severe disabilities. The majority of us fall somewhere in between the two. Again, God's hand is sovereign in His creation of each and every individual; and every person has something unique that God would have them do. Whatever it is for each of your children, teach them to do it heartily for the Lord. Teach them to put effort and self-discipline into it. God has gifted them. What a joy it is to discover what they have been gifted with and then watch them use it to the best of their ability for His glory.

- Read all of I Corinthians 12.

- Romans 12:11: *Never be lacking in zeal, but keep your spiritual fervor, serving the Lord.*

- Ephesians 2:10: *For we are God's workmanship, created in Christ Jesus to do good works, which God prepared in advance for us to do.*

- Ephesians 6:7: *Serve wholeheartedly, as if you were serving the Lord, not men...*

- Philippians 2:13: *For it is God who works in you to will and to act according to his good purpose.*

- Colossians 3:23-24: *Whatever you do, work at it with all your heart, as working for the Lord, not for men, since you know that you will receive an inheritance from the Lord as a reward. It is the Lord Christ you are serving.*

- 1 Peter 4:10-11: *Each one should use whatever gift he has received to serve others, faithfully administering God's grace in its various forms. If anyone speaks, he should do it as one speaking the very words of God. If anyone serves, he should do it with the strength God provides, so that in all things God may be praised through Jesus Christ. To him be the glory and the power forever and ever. Amen.*

USING GIFTS WITH HUMILITY

How we view our gifts and talents is of paramount importance. Thankfully, we have a marvelous model to follow. Jesus is perfect in every way and transcendent over all humanity, yet when He came to live among us, he came to be a servant. He emptied himself of all His heavenly glories, took on the frame of a man, and willingly gave of His life for us. Encourage your children to model themselves after the humble, other-oriented, servant heart of the Lord Jesus, not a self-serving society.

As your children grow and develop, teach them to guard their hearts against a proud and haughty spirit. Let them see each gift and talent as a tool given by God for the purpose of serving God. Show them by example how to seek to glorify God, not self, in all they do – just as Jesus did.

- Read and discuss Daniel 4:28-37.

- Jeremiah 9:23-24: *This is what the Lord says: "Let not the wise man boast of his wisdom, or the strong man boast of his strength or the rich man boast of his riches, but let **him** who boasts boast about this: that he understands and knows me, that I am the Lord, who exercises kindness, justice and righteousness on earth, for in these I delight," declares the Lord.*

- Matthew 11:29: *Take my yoke upon you and learn from me, for I am gentle and humble in heart, and you will find rest for your souls.*

- 2 Corinthians 3:5: *Not that we are competent in ourselves to claim anything for ourselves, but our competence comes from God.*

- Ephesians 4:1-2: *As a prisoner for the Lord, then, I urge you to live a life worthy of the calling you have received. Be completely humble and gentle; be patient, bearing with one another in love.*

- Philippians 2:5-8: *Your attitude should be the same as that of Christ Jesus: who, being in very nature God, did not consider equality with God something to be grasped, but made himself nothing, taking the very nature of a servant, being made in human likeness. And being found in appearance as a man, he humbled himself and became obedient to death – even death on a cross!*

- 1 Peter 5:6: *Humble yourselves, therefore, under God's mighty hand, that he may lift you up in due time.*

THE RACE WORTH RUNNING

The runners take their marks. Muscles tense. The crack of a gun splits the air, and they are off! Sprinting forward, the trained athletes set their sights on the goal and strain towards the finish line. Who will win…?

Life can seem like a race much of the time. Worldly influences can make it feel like you are being surrounded by a throng of marathon runners. Each person is racing to the finish line, trying to come in first or at least respectably close; trying to find a basis for personal value and self-worth. The "Olympians" in this worldly race of life are often defined by qualities such as intellect, looks, ability and wealth. Do you find yourself and your children occasionally joining in the worldly race?

Some Christians join the throng and struggle against the ever-increasing pressures to succeed against odds that forever mount before them. In contrast, some people feel they can never compete. It is just too difficult; the competition is too stiff and overwhelming. Sadly, they sit on the sidelines and watch, wishing to be out on the track.

Whether you are on the racetrack or off on the sidelines, life eventually reveals that either position will always be disappointing and unfulfilling. Why? Because the inherent value of the race is without foundation, its basis for winning is superficial and its rewards are temporal. Even the apparent winners in this race have their lonely moments when the thrill of their triumph is over. They know that their momentary victory can be easily swept away and lost. For instance:

If worth is based on:

Looks: Beauty will fade away, it will never be flawless, and there will always be someone prettier or more handsome.

Sports: Victory or defeat is only one game or competition away. A person can be injured and unable to play. There will always be someone better. You will get old!

Wealth: Money and other assets can be easily lost, and there will always be an unquenchable desire for more. Money never satisfies and it "cannot buy happiness."

Speaking, music, art, drama, and intelligence: The sense of achievement in these areas is fleeting. The bright moments in the limelight may appear suddenly and then just as rapidly fade away into obscurity.

Clearly, the race towards these things and all other human aspirations will never completely satisfy the quest for meaning and worth. They will never relieve the inner longing of the soul. They are deceitful counterfeits of what will really satisfy the human heart.

So then, what is the answer? The answer is this: **We don't have to run in this race!** God does not want His children striving and competing in this world's system to find significance. He wants us finding worth and fulfillment in *Him*. We are already fully loved and accepted by Him. *We are already winners!* Cease from striving and rest in Him! He wants us all to quit looking inside ourselves for value and instead, look heavenward and see the incredible worth that we have already been given by God! He *alone* is the truly satisfying and authentic source of our worth. He alone can relieve the inner longings of our souls.

Consider the words of the prophet Jeremiah:

Jeremiah 2:13: *My people have committed two sins: They have forsaken Me, the spring of living water, and have dug their own cisterns, broken cisterns that cannot hold water.*

Water is a vital necessity that all humans require to survive. Not only do our bodies need this life-giving water, but the Scriptures speak of a thirst within our own souls. Jeremiah tells of how God provided his people with water; yet they turned from a spring of living water to a cistern that they had dug with their own hands. A cistern is not like a well; it is not a *source* of water. It is merely a holding tank. It must be filled with rainwater or collected by some other means for storage.

Why would a person turn his back from a bubbling, clean, clear spring of living water and go to the trouble of collecting water from another source? Then, after all the trouble of drawing and carrying the water, why put it into a broken cistern that leaks and causes the precious water to seep into the ground?

What a foolish waste of effort to have worked so hard to keep a broken cistern filled with water. Yet when we seek to find worth and fulfillment in worldly aspirations, and try so hard to keep them satisfying our thirsty souls, we are doing just that: pouring buckets of water, hauled with great difficulty, into a broken, cracked, and leaky cistern. In contrast, how refreshing and invigorating it is when we simply turn back to the clear, bubbling spring of living water and take a long drink.

The Bible says that Jesus is the source of living water. He *alone* can quench the thirst in our souls. When we drink from Him, we will never thirst. Our innermost being will *always* be satisfied. From the satisfaction that wells up with us, we will have the energy to use our gifts and talents (whatever they may be), to *minister* to those around us and to glorify our Father in heaven. There is no greater source of abundant joy and fulfillment!

Consider these verses from the Scriptures:

- **Psalms 16:11**: *Thou wilt make known to me the path of life. In thy presence is fullness of joy; In thy right hand there are pleasures forever. (NASB)*

- **Psalm 42:1-2a**: *As the deer pants for streams of water, so my soul pants for you, O God. My soul thirsts for God, for the living God.*

- **John 4:14**: *...whoever drinks the water I give him will never thirst. Indeed, the water I give him will become in him a spring of water welling up to eternal life.*

- **1 John 3:1a**: *How great is the love the Father has lavished on us, that we should be called children of God! And that is what we are!*

- **1 Peter 2:9**: *But you are a chosen people, a royal priesthood, a holy nation, a people belonging to God, that you may declare the praises of Him who called you out of darkness into His wonderful light.*

- **Colossians 3:17**: *Therefore, "whatever you do, whether in word or deed, do it all in the name of the Lord Jesus, giving thanks to God the Father through him."*

- **Matthew 5:16**: *In the same way, let your light shine before men, that they may see your good deeds and praise your Father in heaven.*

If we are not to run in this worldly marathon, does that leave us aimless, drifting and without direction? Absolutely not! For there still is a race to be run, and this is the race *worth* running. In the New Testament, Paul speaks of this very special race; however, it is on a very different track. Our race is not for the purposes of winning against another opponent. Rather, it is a race run with courage and determination in order to accomplish God's purpose in our lives and to further His glorious kingdom. Every gift, skill and ability, every career and calling is encompassed in this race. As we run, wherever we run, we share the good news of His love, grace and gift of salvation. We become salt and light in our families, our community and our world. In so doing, we bring praise, exaltation and glory to God in heaven.

Note Paul's words:

- **Acts 20:24:** *However, I consider my life worth nothing to me, if only I may finish the race and complete the task the Lord Jesus has given me – the task of testifying to the gospel of God's grace.*

- **1 Corinthians 9:24-25:** *Do you not know that in a race all the runners run, but only one gets the prize? Run in such a way as to get the prize. Everyone who competes in the games goes into strict training. They do it to get a crown that will not last; but we do it to get a crown that will last forever.*

- **2 Timothy 4:7-8:** *I have fought the good fight, I have finished the race, I have kept the faith. Now there is in store for me the crown of righteousness, which the Lord, the righteous Judge, will award to me on that day – and not only to me, but also to all who have longed for his appearing.*

- **Hebrews 12:1:** *Therefore, since we are surrounded by such a great cloud of witnesses, let us throw off everything that hinders and the sin that so easily entangles, and let us run with perseverance the race marked out for us.*

In conclusion, the Christian life has aim, direction and purpose. It is to be lived with intensity and determination, empowered by the indwelling of the Holy Spirit. Each gift and talent humbly acknowledged is used to fulfill the glorious will of God. For the believer, every new day presents a new challenge, causing us to persevere, to grow, to serve, to love and to become more like our precious Lord and Savior, Jesus Christ.

God has a beautiful design for our lives.
It can only be found when we
find our worth in Him and
acknowledge that He has gifted us
and equipped us
to serve Him.

We need to love Him.
Humbly give Him our best.
Serve Him, rest in Him,
and give Him
the Glory.

Chapter Four

Biblical Character Traits

ᴀ☙❧ᴀ

C hristian parents earnestly desire biblical character traits in their children, but sometimes it is unclear as to just what these character traits are and how children are supposed to learn them. Unfortunately, there is no quick and easy way for them to obtain these virtuous qualities. It is a long-term process not only for children to gain them, but for parents as well. It is a process that continues throughout an entire lifetime. Therefore, it is not your job to demand the end product of good character from your children; instead you should lead them on the road that they must travel, and guide them as far as you possibly can. After that point they must travel it alone. God, through His Word, and through the prompting of His Spirit will continue to be at work in their lives. For it is God's desire that:

"...we all reach unity in the faith and in the knowledge of the Son of God and become mature, attaining to the whole measure of the fullness of Christ." Ephesians 4:13

During your child rearing years, your example will be a primary influence in your children's lives. Consider the following poem:

A careful man I ought to be;
a little fellow follows me.
I do not dare to go astray,
for fear he'll go the selfsame way.

Not once can I escape his eyes:
Whate'er he sees me do he tries.

Like me he says he's going to be,
that little chap who follows me.

I must remember as I go
Through summer sun and winter snow,
I'm molding for the years to be –
That little chap who follows me.
Author unknown

Modeling the Christian life is by far one of the most difficult parts of parenting, and it can only done as you seek the strength and wisdom of God. For if you teach one thing with your mouth and do something else with your life, your children will see your hypocrisy; they may ultimately rebel against your authority and the principles you have taught them. Can parents be perfect examples? No. Parents sin, too. Nevertheless, when we do, we can teach by example how to repent, to seek forgiveness, and to correct our wrongs as best we can. Children need to see that as well.

In addition to the example you seek to set, you can never underestimate the importance of prayer for your children. Your prayers on behalf of your children come before the very throne of God and can be sent heavenward as long as God gives you breath. God alone knows, this side of heaven, what the petitions made by faithful parents have wrought in the lives of their children. So do not lose heart. Be faithful to lead by example, teach little by little, and do not fail to pray. Remember that God loves your children more than you do. He is just as much interested in the *process* of their development as He is in the final *product*. This is true not just in your children's lives, but in yours as well.

Character is never developed in a vacuum. You cannot build endurance, perseverance or become a hard worker if you have nothing to do. You cannot develop kindness, if you do not know what it is or how and when it is to be shown. It is only through the convicting work of the Holy Spirit, the practical application of biblical principles, and the patient training of parents, that good character will begin to evolve. You will have the joy of seeing it displayed throughout the day-to-day situations of life, especially in an atmosphere of encouragement, acceptance and love.

As Christians, godly character is an essential expression of our faith. It displays our redeemed nature that is in the process of being conformed into the image of Jesus Christ. Christlike character traits, exhibited in our lives and in the lives of our children, enable us to be salt and light in this world. When you see your children demonstrate godly character, express your appreciation and praise them for it. Words of praise and encouragement go a very long way in reinforcing right behavior in children. Bathe them regularly in it!

In this chapter on Character Traits you will find the following sections:

> Developing Character
> Character Traits
> Bible Characters to Consider
> Becoming Godly Men and Women
> Treasures for the Young

Many aspects of this chapter could be used effectively for family devotions. For instance:

- Open your Bibles together, read and discuss the Scripture references along with the character traits listed.
- Discuss practical ways to develop different character traits.
- Reflect on how God's Word gives wise counsel that is as practical today as when it was written.
- Talk about God's wise design for men and women and the blessings that result when we follow His guiding principles.
- Observe the biblical models of real people who exhibited both good character and bad.
- Discuss how faith and obedience to God, or the lack thereof, directly influenced the development of their character, how they lived their lives, and what they are remembered for today.
- Finally, ask your children what kind of character traits they want to exhibit, and how they want to be remembered by future generations.

DEVELOPING CHARACTER

Developing Christlike character is a lifelong process. Identifying and defining these traits will be the first step on the path of your training.

To aid you in motivating your children in a positive direction during this process, it helps to assure that every aspect of teaching and training should be as enjoyable an experience as possible. For example, be quick to say, "What an excellent example of self-control (or other trait) you are showing! I am so proud of you. This pleases God too!" (You can even teach your children to take notice and encourage one another as well.)

To help you in this training process, you might want to make a copy of the "Character Traits" list for each of your children. Put their names on the top of the list. As you study each character trait, and as you see them emerge in their lives, show your recognition by placing a gold star sticker over the printed star in each section. This will help them to clearly identify the trait, get excited about their progress and continue to build on it.

Above all, train them to depend on the indwelling power of the Holy Spirit as they strive toward virtuous behavior. Having well behaved children is a nice thing, but it is far better to have children with godly character who seek to live holy and pure lives because it is right and because they desire to please God with all their hearts.

As you study the following list together:
- Discuss the definition of each trait.
- Read and consider the scripture references.
- Think of situations or people that exhibit that particular trait.
- Act out an example of how this character trait can be displayed.
- Encourage them with praise when you find evidence of a trait already in their lives.
- Remind them that their true character is revealed in how they act when no one is watching.

CHARACTER TRAITS

The path of the righteous is like the first gleam of dawn, shining ever brighter till the full light of day. Proverbs 4:18

* Alert: Watchful, aware, prepared for action – Prov. 4:20-27; 1 Thess. 5:6-8; 1 Peter 1:13; 5:8-11

* Compassionate: Sympathetic and tender toward those who suffer and a yearning to alleviate their pain or sorrow – Eph. 4:32; Phil. 2:1-4; Col. 3:12-14; 1 Peter 3:8-9

* Content: Serene satisfaction and gratefulness with your circumstances and with what you possess – Prov. 14:30; Matt. 6:25-34; Phil 4:11-13; 1 Tim. 6:6-10; Heb. 13:5

* Cooperative: Willing to share, participate, and work alongside others toward common goals and purposes – Rom. 15:5-6; Eph. 4:3-6; Phil. 1:27; 2:1-2

* Courageous: Bold and brave; willing to take risks in order to do what is right – Prov. 3:25-26; 28:1; 29:25; 1 Cor. 16:13; Eph. 6:10-20; Phil 1:20-21; 2 Tim. 1:7

* Diligent: Hardworking, keeps to the task and finishes it – Prov. 10:4; 13:4; 21:5; 1 Tim. 4:11-16; 2 Tim. 2:2,15

* Discerning: Showing good judgment, able to understand and choose right from wrong – Prov. 3:21-24; 16:21; 17:24; 18:15; Phil. 1:9-11; 1 John 2:15-18

* Encourager: One who gives support to others by inspiring faith, courage, hope and confidence – Prov. 12:25; 16:24; 22:11; Eph. 4:29; 1 Thess. 5:11-14; Heb. 3:13; 10:23-25

* **Enduring:** Bearing up steadfastly in suffering; patient under pressure and when circumstances are difficult – Isaiah 40:31; Rom. 5:1-5; 8:17; 2 Cor. 4:7-9, 16-18; Heb. 12:1-3; James 1:2-4; 1 Pet. 4:12-16

* **Faithful:** Devoted, reliable, loyal, trustworthy and conscientious – Ruth 1:14-18; 2:11-12; Prov. 3:3-4; 14:22; Rom. 12:10; 2 Tim 2:2; Titus 3:8; 1 Peter 4:10

* **Forgiving:** Willing to pardon another's offense without holding a grudge – Prov. 17:9; Matt. 18:21-22; Luke 17:3-4; Eph. 4:32; Col. 3:13-14

* **Generous:** Unselfish, willing to share what God has given; a cheerful giver – Psalms 112:5-7; Prov. 3:9-10, 27-28; 19:17; 22:9; Matt. 6:2-4; 2 Cor. 9:6-15

* **Gentle:** Mild, soothing and peaceful in thoughts, words and actions – Prov. 15:1; Gal. 6:1; Eph. 4:1-2; Phil 4:5; 1 Peter 3:3-4

* **Good:** Seeks to do what is morally excellent, virtuous, and beneficial – Prov. 3:27; 14:14; Rom. 12:9; 2 Cor. 9:8; Gal. 6:10; Col. 1:10; 1 Peter 3:13

* **Holy:** Dedicated and devoted to loving and serving God; set apart from the world; pure and reverent – Rom. 12:1; Eph. 1:4; 1 Thess. 4:7; 2 Tim. 2:20-21; 1 Peter 1:14-16; 2:9-12

* **Hopeful:** Trusting and confident of God's sovereign and personal involvement in our lives and on our eternal salvation which is assured by faith – Psalm 62:5-8; 130:5; 147:11; Prov. 23:17-18; 1 Thess. 1:2-3; 1 Tim. 6:17; 2 Peter 3:13-14

* **Hospitable:** Warm and gracious towards others, whether they are strangers, friends, or family; an open home and heart – Matt. 25:34-40; Mark 9:41; Rom. 12:13; Heb. 13:2; James 2:15-16; 1 Peter 4:9-10

* **Humble:** Modest and unpretentious; doesn't seek personal acclaim – Prov. 11:2; 15:33; 26:12; Phil. 2:3-11; James 4:7-17; 1 Peter 5:5-6

* **Initiating:** Able to take the first step; enthusiastic; sees what needs to be done and does it without being asked; a leader in doing what is right – Prov. 6: 6-8; 19:2; 2 Cor. 9:2; Col. 4:5

* **Joyful:** A glad heart assured of God's goodness in all circumstances – Prov. 15:13,30; 17:22; Rom. 12:12; 15:13; Phil. 4:4-7; 1 Thess. 5:16; 1 Peter 4:12-13

* **Just:** Concerned with all that is fair, upright, and equitable in respect to others – Psalms 37:28; 106:3; Prov. 2: 1,2,9,10; 16:8; 21:15; 24:23-25; Micah 6:8

* **Kind:** Actively pursuing actions that are welcoming, courteous and of benefit to others – Prov. 12:25; 14:31; 19:17; 1 Cor. 13:4; Eph. 4:32; 1 Thess. 5:15; 2 Peter 1:5-7

* **Listener:** One who focuses their full attention on the words, actions and feelings of someone else – Prov. 10:19; 13:3; 17:28; 18:2,13; 19:20; 25:12; 29:20

* **Loving:** A deep affection, commitment, and faithfulness expressed in words and actions – Prov. 16:7; 21:21; Rom. 13:8-10; 1 Cor. 13; Eph. 5:25-29; Phil. 1:9-11; 1 John 4:7-21

* **Obedient:** Following and completing instructions given by someone in authority – promptly, cheerfully and without complaint – Prov. 30:17; Eph. 6:1-3, 5-8; 1 John 2:3-6; 3:21-24; 2 John 4-6

* **Orderly:** Neat, methodical, organized; good manager and planner – Prov. 14:22; 15:22; 16:3; 19:21; 21:5

* **Patient:** Inner strength, and composure when experiencing misfortune, annoying situations, and suffering; a quiet trust in the Lord and His perfect timing in all things; willing to wait and accept others who do things differently than you would – Prov. 14:29; 15:18; 16:32; 19:11; Eph. 4:2; Col. 3:12-13

* **Peacemaker:** A mediator or go-between who seeks resolution and restoration in relationships that are in conflict – Psalm 37:37; Prov. 12:20; Matt. 5:9; Rom. 12:18; Col. 3:15; James 3:17-18; 1 Peter 3:8-9

* **Persevering:** Persistent and steadfast in a challenging task despite difficulty or obstacles – 1 Cor. 13:6-7; Gal 6:9; Phil. 3:12-14; Heb. 12:1; James 1:12; 2 Peter 1:5-11

* **Prayerful:** Regularly and consistently speaking to God with words of adoration, confession, thanksgiving and supplication (ACTS); faithfully interceding for others in need – Matt. 6:5-13; Eph. 6: 18-20; Phil. 4:6; Col. 4:2-4; 1 Thess. 5:16-18; James 5:16; 1 John 5:14-15

* **Pure:** Cleanliness in heart, mind, body, speech, and actions – Prov. 20:11; 1 Cor. 6:18-20; Eph. 4:29; 5:3-4; Phil. 2:14-15; 4:8; 1 Tim. 4:12; 2 Tim. 2:22; 1 Peter 3:3-4

* **Respectful:** Desiring to show favor or honor to another; courteous and polite – Lev. 19:32; Rom. 12:10; Eph.6: 2; 5:33b; 1 Tim. 5:1-2, 17; 1 Pet. 2:17; 3:7

* **Self-Controlled:** Self-disciplined and discrete; uses wise self-restraint over emotions and actions – Prov. 17:27-28; 18:7; 22:24-25; 29:11; Eph. 4:26-27; 2 Tim. 1:7; James 1:19-20, 26

* **Servant-Hearted:** Helpful and willing to share time, money, and abilities with others in need – Gal. 6:10; Eph 2:10; 4:11-13; 6:7-8; Col. 3:23-24; 1 Peter 4:10

* **Submissive:** Willing to yield or defer to someone else's judgment, opinion, or decision – Rom. 13:1-7; Eph. 5:21-24; Heb. 13:17; 1 Peter 2:13-15, 18-20

* **Teachable:** Humbly receives instruction, pursues knowledge and understanding, and faithfully seeks to apply what is learned – Deut. 4:5-11; Psalm 119:9-16, 33-37, 44-48, 66-68, 71, 130; Prov. 1:8-9; 4:1-4; Matt. 11:29; Phil. 4:9; 2 Tim. 2:2

* **Thankful:** Consistently expresses gratefulness and appreciation to God and others – Psalm 100; 2 Cor. 2:14; Phil. 4:4-7; Col. 1:9-14; 2:6-7; 3:15-17; 1 Thess. 5:16-18; Heb. 12:28

* **Truthful:** Speaks honestly; communicates facts with accuracy; admits personal error – Prov. 12:19, 22; 14:5; 24:26; Eph. 4:25

* **Wise:** Discerning and judging properly as to what is true and right; biblical application of knowledge and understanding – Prov. 2:1-15; 3:13-18; 8:11; 10:1, 11:2; 12:15,18; 13:20, 15:31; 18:15; 23:23; 24:3-4; Daniel 12:3; 1 Cor. 3:18-20; Eph. 5:15-16; James 3:13-18

But the fruit of the Spirit is love, joy, peace, patience, kindness, goodness, faithfulness, gentleness and self-control. Against such things there is no law. Galatians 5:22-23

For this very reason, make every effort to add to your faith goodness; and to goodness, knowledge; and to knowledge, self-control; and to self-control, perseverance; and to perseverance, godliness; and to godliness, brotherly kindness; and to brotherly kindness, love. 2 Peter 1:5-7

As water reflects a face, So a man's heart reflects the man. Proverbs 27:19

BIBLE CHARACTERS TO CONSIDER
Studying the people mentioned in the Bible is a wonderful way to see character in action, both right and wrong. Included here are some individuals from the Bible for your consideration. Your children may already be aware of the stories about their lives. If not, you may want to read a Bible story book to acquaint yourselves with them or use the referenced passages from the Scriptures. Discuss what are the right as well as the wrong character traits that were exhibited in their lives. Think about the blessings they experienced when they did what was right and the consequences when they did what was wrong. Note that God is able to use imperfect people, just like the rest of us, to accomplish His plan. Space is given for you to make notes of your observations.

As you read, ask yourselves:
- From the previous list of Character Traits, which traits can you identify in the lives of the following people?
- Which traits are they lacking?
- What was their faith in God like?
- How did God use them?
- What were the consequences or blessings resulting from their actions?
- What are they remembered for today?
- How does my knowledge of their lives change the way I think or behave?

Adam and Eve: Genesis 2:4-4:26:

Cain and Able: Genesis 4:1-16:

Noah: Genesis 5:28-9:17:

Abraham: Genesis 11:26-18:33; 20-24; 25:1-11; Hebrews 11:8-19:

Jacob: Genesis 25:19-34, 27-35; 45:25-48:22; 49:29-50:14; Hebrews 11:21:

Joseph: Genesis 30:22-24; 37:1-36; 39:1-50:26; Hebrews 11:22:

Moses: Exodus 1:1-20:21; 31:18-34:35; Numbers 10:29-14:45; 16:1-17:13; 20:1-13; 27:12-23; Hebrews 11:24-29:

Joshua: Numbers 11:26-29; 13:16-14:9; 27:18-23; Joshua 1; 5:13-6:27; 8:30-35; 24:1-33:

Esther: Book of Esther:

Ruth and Naomi: Book of Ruth:

Saul: 1 Samuel, chapters 9-11; 13-20; 24; 26; 28; 31:

David: 1 Samuel 16-31; 2 Samuel 1-24; 1 Kings 1-2:12; Acts 13:21-22:

Uriah: 2 Samuel 11-12:23:

Solomon: 1 Kings 1:28-3:28; 4:20-6:1; 8-11:

Josiah: 2 Kings 22:1-23:30:

Daniel: Daniel chapters 1-6:

Job: Job chapters 1-2; 42:

Judas Iscariot: Matthew 10:2-4; 26:14-16; 27:1-10; Mark 14:41-46; John 12:1-7; 13:21-30:

Peter: Matthew 4:18-20; 10:2-4; 14:22-32; 16:13-20; 17:1-8; 26:31-35; 26:69-75; Mark 14:27-31, 66-72; Luke 5:1-11; 22:60-62; John 20:1-9; 21:1-25; Acts 1:12-5:42; 9:32-12:19:

John the Baptist: Matthew 3:1-17; 11:1-19; 14:1-12; Mark 1:1-15; 6:14-29; Luke 1:1-80; 3:1-22; John 3:22-36:

Paul: Acts 7:54-8:3; 9:1-30; 11:22-30; 12-28:

Jesus: Discuss what has been recorded about Jesus in the New Testament Gospels (Matthew, Mark, Luke and John)

BECOMING GODLY MEN AND WOMEN

These lists of verses from the Bible are specific to boys and girls (who will soon be men and women, as well as husbands and wives). With your Bibles, look them up together and discuss why these verses are important and how each one can be applied to their lives. Remember to emphasis the *process* of your child's walk with God, not merely the results. It is not performance that is paramount, rather it is for your child to have a heart that is committed to loving God, delighting in Him and therefore living a life of effective usefulness for His kingdom. This can only happen when a child has accepted Jesus as their Lord and Savior and has been given a new nature that is indwelt by the Holy Spirit. Godliness is the result of a personal relationship with God.

You may want to photocopy these pages so each family member will have his or her own set. Space is given for you to write down your observations.

As you read the following verses ask:

- What does God ask of men or women who follow Him?
- Why is it important to be this way?
- How can I apply this to my life?
- What changes do I need to make?

Traits of a Godly Man

Luke 2:52 (our model):

1 Corinthians 16:13-14:

Ephesians 5:25-33:

Colossians 3:19-21:

1 Timothy 3:1-10:

1 Timothy 3:12-13:

1 Timothy 4:12:

1 Timothy 6:11-12:

Titus 1:5-9:

Titus 2:1-2, 6-8:

1 Peter 3:7:

Traits of a Godly Woman

Proverbs 12:4; 14:1:

Proverbs 31:10-31:

Luke 10:38-42 (observe Mary):

Acts 9:36-43:

Ephesians 5:22-24:

1 Timothy 2:9-12:

1 Timothy 3:11:

Titus 2:3-5:

1 Peter 3:1-6:

TREASURES FOR THE YOUNG
Both young men and young women should take time to study three very important passages that describe our relationship to God and to others: the Ten Commandments, the Beatitudes, and the "Golden Rule." Meditate on these passages. Summarize their commandments and promises, and take notes as you consider these questions:
- How does this describe what my relationship with God is to be like?
- How does this describe what my relationship to others is to be like?
- What are the promises or blessings from God when I follow them?

The Ten Commandments: Exodus 20:1-17:

The Beatitudes: Matthew 5:1-16:

"The Golden Rule": Mark 12:28-31:

In addition to the previous passages, carefully read and study the book of Proverbs. It is a treasure chest filled with wisdom, counsel and guidance. Time spent in this priceless book will be of enormous value in helping your children develop godly character and live a life based upon biblical principles.

Encourage your sons and daughters to keep a journal of personal lessons from the book of Proverbs as well as their personal devotions in general. This will be a tremendous instrument in their spiritual growth. It can be referred to time and time again as they review the lessons that the Lord has taught them.

Godly character:
A rare and priceless flower.
It cannot be bought.
It cannot be sold.
It can only be grown.

The precious seeds are sown,
take root, and bring forth a lovely blossom.
May your children surround you
as a beautiful bouquet.

Chapter Five

Manners

"Let's mind our manners!" I'm sure that everyone has heard that saying more than once while growing up. But, why do we? Basically, minding our manners makes us all easier to be around. Manners are what oil the cogs of human interaction. Manners are a way of communicating to others that they are *important* and of great *value*. Without them people would always be acting like...well...just use your imagination.

Parents have no way of knowing where their children will be or what they will be doing in the future. The options are limitless. Your child may become an ambassador for your country, a missionary in a foreign land, a pastor, or president – appearing before monarchs, heads of state, congregations, or jungle tribes. He or she may become an executive, computer technician, mechanic, teacher, doctor, nurse, mom or dad. Wherever it is that the Lord leads them, children need to be prepared to behave in such a way that their message of Christ's love is unhindered. Their manners in various situations will be shown in what they say, how they dress, or how politely they eat the unfamiliar foods placed before them.

As you teach these different acts of courtesy, remember that this is a process. As a baby learns to walk one step at a time, so it is in many other areas of life. Don't be discouraged if your children forget what seems obvious to you, and they make an etiquette *faux pas*. Just smile, remind them of what they forgot, and carry on.

Many guidelines are written down in the following pages, however it is impossible for rules of behavior for every possible situation to be documented or remembered. Whatever is not "specifically" taught to your children can be governed by the principles given in the Scriptures. There are three excellent passages in God's Word which provide an umbrella that helps cover most of the situations your children will ever encounter:

Matthew 7:12: *So in everything, do to others what you would have them do to you.*

Mark 12:31: *Love your neighbor as yourself.*

Romans 12:10: *Be devoted to one another in brotherly love. Honor one another above yourselves.*

Not only does the Bible give us guidance in regards to our behavior, but it is also from the Scriptures that we can observe the life of Christ, who is our greatest role model. In addition, it is by the Spirit of God that our hearts are prompted to holy and righteous living. I fully believe that Christians, above all others, should be the most gracious, hospitable, and mannerly group of people on the face of the earth.

Onward to gracious living....

GRACIOUS LIVING FROM GOD'S WORD

The Bible is the most important foundation we have in our lives to guide us into gracious living. To use the following lists, spend time together as a family and share these verses from God's Word.

As you read through these verses, ask questions such as:
- Does it speak to you or me personally?
- What are specific behaviors needed to fulfill what God wants me to do?
- Why is it important for me to do this?
- When I fail to follow this principle, what will be the result?
- How does this verse affect the way I treat other people?

Read all of Proverbs 3

Proverbs 4:20-27: *My son, pay attention to what I say: listen closely to my words. Do not let them out of your sight, keep them within your heart; for they are life to those who find them and health to a man's whole body. Above all else, guard your heart for it is the wellspring of life. Put away perversity from your mouth; keep corrupt talk far from your lips. Let your eyes look straight ahead, fix your gaze directly before you. Make level paths for your feet and take only ways that are firm. Do not swerve to the right or the left; keep your foot from evil.*

Proverbs 15:1: *A gentle answer turns away wrath, but a harsh word stirs up anger.*

Proverbs 22:24: *Do not make friends with a hot-tempered man, do not associate with one easily angered, or you may learn his ways and get yourself ensnared.*

Proverbs 29:11: *A fool gives full vent to his anger, but a wise man keeps himself under control.*

Ephesians 4:26: *In your anger do not sin. Do not let the sun go down while you are still angry.*

Matthew 7:12: *So in everything, do to others what you would have them do to you...*

Galatians 5:22-23: *For the fruit of the Spirit is love, joy, peace, patience, kindness, goodness, faithfulness, gentleness and self-control. Against such things there is no law.*

Ephesians 4:32: *Be kind and compassionate to one another, forgiving each other, just as in Christ God forgave you.*

Ephesians 4:29: *Do not let any unwholesome talk come out of your mouths, but only what is helpful for building others up according to their needs, that it may benefit those who listen.*

Ephesians 5:1: *Be imitators of God therefore, as dearly loved children.*

Ephesians 5:21: *Submit to one another out of reverence for Christ.*

Ephesians 6:1: *Children obey your parents in the Lord, for this is right. Honor your father and mother which is the first commandment with a promise – that it may go well with you and that you may enjoy long life on the earth.*

Philippians 1:27: *Whatever happens, conduct yourselves in a manner worthy of the gospel of Christ.*

Philippians 2:3: *Do nothing from selfish ambition or vain conceit, but in humility consider others better than yourselves.*

Philippians 2:14-15: *Do everything without complaining or arguing so that you may become blameless and pure, children of God in a crooked and depraved generation, in which you shine like stars in the universe…*

Philippians 4:4-5: *Rejoice in the Lord always. I will say it again: Rejoice! Let your gentleness be evident to all. The Lord is near.*

Philippians 4:8: *Finally brothers, whatever is true, whatever is noble, whatever is right, whatever is pure, whatever is lovely, whatever is admirable – if anything is excellent or praiseworthy think about such things.*

Colossians 1:10-12: *And we pray this in order that you may live a life worthy of the Lord and may please him in every way: bearing fruit in every good work, growing in the knowledge of God, being strengthened with all power according to his glorious might so that you may have great endurance and patience, and joyfully giving thanks to the Father, who has qualified you to share in the inheritance of the saints in the kingdom of light.*

Colossians 3:12-13: *Therefore, as God's chosen people, holy and dearly loved, clothe yourselves with compassion, kindness, humility, gentleness and patience. Bear with each other and forgive whatever grievances you may have against one another. Forgive as the Lord forgave you. And over all these virtues put on love, which binds them all together in perfect unity.*

2 Peter 4:9-10: *Offer hospitality to one another without grumbling. Each one should use whatever gift he has received to serve others, faithfully administering God's grace in its various forms.*

1 Timothy 4:12: *Don't let anyone look down on you because you are young, but set an example for the believers in speech, in life, in love, in faith and in purity.*

Proverbs 20:11: *Even a child is knows by his actions, by whether his conduct is pure and right.*

Of course, there is much more in the Scriptures that gives guidance in the area of gracious living. As mentioned previously, a verse-by-verse reading and discussion of Proverbs during family devotions is a delightful study in the area of wisdom and right living.

LIST OF SPECIFIC MANNERS

As you begin using the "List of Specific Manners," you may start from the beginning or choose a topic that you feel would be the most beneficial for your family right now. Begin reading through the "rules," covering just a few at a time. You will notice that there are scripture verses listed along with several of the manners rules. Incorporate them into your study. Have your children look up and read the verses. Then discuss how the principles of Scripture apply. Focus on certain principles for a day or a week, continually reinforcing them in your daily experiences. (Start slow so you don't overwhelm your children or yourself!) Once your children show that they have a good, practical understanding of one set of guidelines, move on and learn new ones. Check the boxes for those you have read and periodically go back and review what you have covered before.

The list of specific manners is divided up in the following categories:

Mannerly Attitudes and Actions
When You Have Guests
When You are the Guest
In Your Own Home
Communication
Ways to Resolve Conflict
For Gentlemen Only
For Ladies Only
Shopping
Traveling
Appearance
Mealtimes
At Church
Miscellaneous Moments

MANNERLY ATTITUDES AND ACTIONS

NAME OF CHILD _____

When you have taught through the attitudes or actions listed below, put a checkmark in the box next to it. Be sure to periodically review what you have learned. You can make a copy of this list for each of your children.

☐ Never say anything to anyone that could hurt someone's feelings – such as teasing, name-calling or insulting. (Matt. 7:12; Eph. 4:29)

☐ If someone makes a mistake, or seems different than you, never point, laugh at or tease them; instead try to make them feel better by showing kindness and acceptance.

☐ Frequently use words like, "Please," "Thank you," "You're welcome," "I'm sorry," "I was wrong," "Will you forgive me?" and "I forgive you." Be sure you mean what you say. (Prov. 22:11)

☐ Never use your fists or sarcastic, cutting comments because you are angry with someone. Learn to work out your differences with appropriate words. You may need to excuse yourself from a tense situation to cool off, and then return later to discuss the problem with the goal of resolving your differences and restoring your relationship. (Prov. 20:22, 29:11; Eph. 4:26; James 1:19-20)

☐ Always speak the truth. (Prov. 12:22; 15:4; 16:13; 24:26)

☐ Love and honor your mom and dad. (Eph. 6:2)

☐ Love your brothers and sisters, and be best friends – not just in private – but in public as well. (John 13:34; Rom. 12:10)

☐ Respectfully address those who are your elders with their proper titles, such as: Mr., Mrs., Miss, Doctor, Professor, or Pastor. Children should not address older people by their first names. ("Older" people are around age 20 or more.) (Rom. 12:10)

❑ When meeting someone for the first time, always smile, look them in the eyes and put out your right hand to shake theirs. Introduce yourself and say, "Hello, my name is David Martin. It is nice to meet you." Then they can say, "Hello, David. My name is Mr. Smith. It is nice to meet you, too." (Role-playing this is helpful and fun!)

❑ If you didn't hear someone clearly, say, "Pardon me?" or "I'm sorry. I didn't hear you." Avoid saying, "Huh?"

❑ Respect other people's conversations and don't walk between two people when they are talking. Go around them.

❑ If someone is walking toward you, step aside and give them room to pass.

❑ When a group of people (a family for instance) is working on a task together, be sure to do your fair share of work (with a cheerful attitude). Don't leave it for someone else to do. (Phil. 2:14)

❑ Show proper respect and good stewardship toward other people's property as well as your own.

❑ Whenever you are out enjoying God's creation of nature, show respect for it; leave it as you found it so those who come after you can enjoy it as well. Always leave park equipment or picnic tables undisturbed. Don't carve in them or leave writing on any public property.

❑ When you borrow something, be sure to return it promptly and make sure it is in as good a shape or better than when you received it.

❑ If you break something that belonged to someone else, admit it promptly. Replace the item or give them the money to replace it.

❑ Respect other people's time:
  1. If you must be somewhere, be punctual and arrive at the scheduled meeting place on time.

2. Do not waste other people's time by dawdling, or neglecting to do your part of a task.

3. Do not waste time in classroom situations by being disruptive to the teacher or to other classmates.

❑ Respect other people's tastes, whether it is in music, art or any other preference (when it is not an issue of sin). You may not like or agree with their tastes, but it is wise to refrain from making negative comments. They may feel that you reject them if you reject their choices. And if they feel rejected by you, you may have lost an opportunity for a good friendship and/or the chance to share your faith in Christ.

❑ When playing games with friends or participating on a team, be a "good sport."

1. Take turns cheerfully.

2. Let others be first.

3. Follow the rules.

4. When picking teams, think of the feelings of those who may not be one of the most "popular" players.

5. Play your best for your team.

6. Don't make fun of others who don't play well or are just learning.

7. Keep playing your best even if you are on the losing team.

8. If you lose, always shake the hands of the winner (or give a high-five) and say a hearty, "Congratulations!"

9. If you are the winner, say, "Thank you" with humble graciousness.

WHEN YOU HAVE GUESTS
(1 Peter 4:9-10; Rom. 12:13)

❑ When you have guests arriving, always go to the door and greet them. Take their coats and hang them up. Let them know how glad you are that they could come.

❑ If an older person comes into the room and there are no seats left, always rise up and offer them your seat. Even if there are other places to sit, make sure that they have the most comfortable one. This shows them honor and respect. (Lev. 19:32)

❑ If your parents have guests, help serve them refreshments. You can also help serve a meal and even offer to assist with the dishes. (1 Peter 4:9-10)

❑ Be a good host or hostess to your guests. Offer to play whatever they would like to play. Offer them snacks and drinks (with your parent's permission). (Phil. 2:3)

❑ Play with all your guests. Don't choose one to play with and ignore the others. This will lead to needlessly hurt feelings. (James 2:1-9)

❑ If a new child has come over to visit with your family for the first time, remember that he may feel more awkward than you do when he is meeting someone new. Extend your hospitality to him and invite him to play with you. Before you know it, you both will have made a new friend.

❑ When playing games with guests, friends or siblings, always play fair. Never cheat, always take turns, and share your toys. (It is okay, though, to set aside toys that are extra special or fragile and not bring those out.) (Prov. 11:4; 1 Tim. 6:18)

❑ Help inform guests as to the house rules, and encourage them to abide by them. Seek out an adult if there is difficulty in this area.

❑ When your guests have to leave, always walk them to the door or to their car, and thank them for coming.

WHEN YOU ARE THE GUEST
(Prov. 25:17; Matt. 7:12; Phil. 2:3; Rom. 12:10)

❑ Thank your host or hostess for inviting you.

❑ Always wipe your feet before you enter the house and remove your shoes if that is their custom. After removing your shoes, put them together neatly and place them out of the way.

❑ Do not handle things in other people's homes unless you politely ask or are given permission to do so.

❑ Keep your hands off walls and windows and your feet off the furniture. This shows respect to your hostess by not leaving dirt and smudges that she will have to clean up when you are gone. (Do the same at your own home!)

❑ Wait to have toys offered to you, or ask politely, instead of reaching out and taking them for yourself.

❑ Never wander around someone's house unless you have been given permission to look around.

❑ When you are a guest, do your best to abide by the house rules of the host family.

❑ When it is time to leave, make sure the toys are put away. Do not leave a mess for your host or hostess (or their children) to clean up. (Parents, if you are all guests in someone's home, be sure to provide your children enough time to do this act of courtesy before you leave.)

❑ Be sure to thank them for inviting you, and let them know you had a very good time. (Be careful to leave at an appropriate time and not overstay your welcome.) (Prov. 25:17)

❑ If you have been invited over to someone's home for a special evening or an extended stay, it is a lovely courtesy to follow up your visit with a kind thank you note expressing your appreciation for their hospitality and friendship.

IN YOUR OWN HOME
(With your own family)

❑ Treat each member in your family as you would your best friend, with courtesy and kindness. (Remember the Wright Brothers. The destiny of the world can be influenced by siblings that work together, love one another, and are committed to encouraging the best in each other.) (Rom. 12:10; 1 Peter 3:8-9)

❑ If someone is resting or sleeping, be considerate to walk, talk and play quietly. (Prov. 27:14)

❑ Never open someone's bedroom door if it is closed. Gently knock and wait for them to answer. Enter only if you have been given permission. (1 Peter 2:17a)

❑ Do not borrow someone's clothes (or other possessions) without asking. (Matt. 7:12; 1 Peter 2:17a)

❑ Be careful to never go through someone's drawers or special cubbyholes without permission. (Matt. 7:12; 1 Peter 2:17a)

❑ Do not read someone else's mail. (Matt. 7:12; 1 Peter 2:17a)

❑ Don't make a mess and leave it for someone else. Always pick up after yourself (socks, shoes, clothes, books, jackets, dishes, toys, towels, etc.).

❑ Keep your own bedroom, or the room you share, clean and orderly out of respect to your parents. This is their house. Keeping clothes and toys put away will make your room a more pleasant place for you (and your sibling) to be, as well as be a place you will not be embarrassed to invite a friend.

❑ Do not read someone's diary without being given permission. (Matt. 7:12; 1 Peter 2:17a)

❑ When watching TV, be aware of the people around you and don't "hog" the TV control. Ask what other people would like to watch. (Matt. 7:12; 1 Peter 2:17a)

❑ Be a prompt responder. If someone calls your name, let him know that you heard. Say, "Yes, Daddy," or "Yes, Suzy, I'm coming." Then come! (Ignoring people is very unmannerly.)

❑ If you see that there is something that needs to be done, do it without being asked. If you are asked to do the task or you promise to do it, follow through. Do it promptly and with a cheerful attitude. (Prov. 19:15; 26:15; 24:30-34)

❑ When you play, use self-control and avoid being overly rough. You might otherwise cause someone to get needlessly hurt. If you do cause someone to get hurt, help him and say, "I'm sorry I hurt you." (And never hurt anyone on purpose!!) (Phil. 4:5)

❑ Use good judgment when playing with others. A person can easily cross over the line from playing a little too rough to being mean. For instance, do not tickle a person till they are hurt or crying. If someone asks you to stop doing something (tickling, wrestling, etc.) then you need to stop immediately.

❑ If you do something wrong, be quick to admit it. Avoid shifting the blame to someone else and making excuses. Apologize and say, "I'm sorry, I was wrong." (And mean it!) Then do whatever you can to correct the situation. (Prov. 28:13)

❑ If someone apologizes to you, be quick to say, "I forgive you." (And mean it!) (Eph. 4:32)

COMMUNICATION
(Col. 4:6)

Carrying on conversations with people you don't know very well can sometimes feel awkward. A helpful skill to learn for these situations is the art of asking questions. If you begin with questions like these you will soon find that you have a lot to talk about.

Questions you can ask:
• What is your name?
• Where do you live?
• What are your hobbies?

- Where do you go to school or work?
- What do you do there?
- Do you enjoy sports? Which ones?

(Be careful to not expect the other person to carry the entire conversation. And don't just talk about yourself.)

❑ Learn to listen before you speak. (Prov. 17:28; 18:2; 18:13; 19:20)

❑ When in a conversation with someone, always listen with *eye contact*.

❑ Always respond when you are spoken to.

❑ Don't brag about yourself. (Prov. 16:18; 27:1-2; Jer. 9:23-24)

❑ Be truthful. (Prov. 12:22; 15:4; 16:13; 24:26)

❑ It is important to speak the truth, but we should not say things that would *unnecessarily* hurt another person, especially when it involves a personal opinion or preference.

❑ Be honest about your own weaknesses (that you expect others to accept). It will make it easier to accept the weaknesses of others. Keeping a sense of humor helps tame a critical spirit too!

❑ Consider your words carefully before you speak. (Prov. 15:4)

❑ Watch your tone of voice. Is it harsh? Sarcastic? Or is it gentle? Seek to be characterized by gentle words. (Prov. 15:1; 25:15; Phil. 4:5)

❑ Eliminate any cursing, coarseness and dirty jokes from your speech. Never use inappropriate gestures or body movements. (Eph. 4:29, 5:3-4)

❑ Whining is not an acceptable way to communicate your needs or wants. Learn to make requests respectfully and in a normal tone of voice. If the request is denied, then calmly and obediently accept the decision of your parent or other adult.

❑ Know the difference between inside and outside voices. Inside voices are quieter; outside voices can be louder. Out of control yelling is impolite and unnecessary. Screaming must be saved for real emergencies. (Prov. 25:28; Prov. 27:14)

❑ Practice self-control over your emotions. Be happy, sad, quiet, even angry, but still maintain self-control. (Titus 2:11-12)

❑ Seek to keep your emotions and expressions appropriate for the situation. There is a time to weep with those who weep, and rejoice with those who rejoice. (Eccl. 3:4)

❑ Seek to maintain a pleasant disposition. Everyone has difficult days now and then, but commit them to the Lord and He can give peace and joy even in the midst of trials. When you are having a significantly hard time, seek out help from those who love and care about you. (Psalm 68:19; Rom. 8:28; Gal. 6:2; James 1:2-4)

❑ Avoid whispering and pointing fingers at other people. It is inconsiderate and can make them feel very uncomfortable.

❑ Don't tell secrets in front of others.

❑ Don't spread mean words about others. That is gossip or possibly slander and it can deeply hurt others. Words that hurt another person can never be taken back. It is always better to not have said them in the first place. (Prov. 10:18-19; 13:3; 1 Peter 3:9)

❑ Friends often like to share harmless, but personal, thoughts and feelings with each other. A trustworthy friend would never tell someone else something of this nature and violate such a special trust.

❑ If someone wants you to keep a confidence (a secret), help your friend understand that confidentiality is a *privilege*, not a "right." If your friend is involved in something illegal, has been victimized, or is doing something potentially harmful to himself or others, let him know that you cannot keep that kind of secret. Let him know that he needs to get help or he needs to stop the harmful behavior. Explain that you are there to support him and that you are willing to go with him and get help as needed. That is how to be a *real* friend.

❑ When you have been given an instruction from an authority (parent, teacher, judge, etc.), it is appropriate that you obey. If your obedience puts you in conflict with another instruction, or if it seems truly inequitable, than you can choose to make a *humble* and *respectable* appeal. (For example: "Mr. Smith, may I appeal to you on this issue?") However, whatever the final decision is, whether the appeal is accepted or denied, you must obey it graciously. (The only exception is when the request would cause you to sin.)

❑ Never interrupt people when they are talking. Simply place your hand on their arm or raise a finger or hand briefly, to let them know you need to speak to them. Then wait till they are done talking and turn to you. If it is urgent that you break in, say, "Excuse me, I'm sorry for interrupting...." The principle is this: be patient and wait for an acceptable opportunity to speak without being rude and interrupting others. (1 Cor. 13:4a)

❑ Know how to properly introduce someone. Say, "Mr. Jones, I would like you to meet my parents, John and Marjorie Smith. Mom and Dad, this is my Sunday school teacher, Mr. Jones." Remember to smile and look each person in the eye. (Role-play this many times until it becomes natural!)

❑ Learn to answer the phone with a *smile in your voice.* (That means you have to answer it with a smile on your face!) A mumbled, or curt "hullo," is very unfriendly. Be a person that someone is glad they called! Say, "Hello, this is the Smith residence," or "Hello, this is Esther Smith." If they want to speak to someone else in the family, say, "Just a moment and I'll get her, may I ask who is calling?" or "I'm sorry, Jesse is not home right now, may I take a message?" Be sure to have paper and pencils by the phone. Write down who called and whom they wanted to talk to, the caller's phone number and what time they called. You may or may not need to write down any other information. (If the child is young, just a name and phone number is a great start!) Then, make sure that your family member gets the message!

❑   If parents are not home when the phone rings, teach your children to say, "I'm sorry, my mom is not able to come to the phone right now. May I have her call you back?" Teach children never to reveal that the parents are not home and never give their phone number and address. They do not need to answer any questions. If a stranger presses for more information, have your children hang up. (It is up to the parents to decide whether children should answer the phone at all if they are not at home. Parents may want to opt to let an answering machine respond.)

❑   If someone calls and they have dialed a wrong number, be kind and polite. Don't make them feel badly for misdialing. (Col. 3:12)

❑   If you call someone and you got a wrong number, do not just hang up the phone. Be gracious and apologize.

❑   When you call a friend on the phone and someone else answers the phone, be courteous and friendly to all your friend's family members. Politely engage them in a friendly greeting such as, "Hello, Mr. Jones, this is Chris Martin. How are you today?" After he answers, proceed to ask for the person you wish to speak to. "May I speak to Jeremy please?"

❑   Do not ever listen in on someone else's telephone conversation. (1 Peter 2:17a)

❑   Remember that people are usually busy at home, so keep your phone calls brief and to the point. Be courteous and say good-bye without belaboring your business. If you want to sit and chat, begin your phone call by asking if they have time to talk, if not, plan a time together when you can visit longer by phone or in person.

WAYS TO RESOLVE CONFLICT
Sadly, it is not uncommon for relationships to be strained when someone says or does something that hurts another person's feelings. If this happens to you,

and your feelings are wounded, it is better to act toward healing the rift rather than to react in anger or become bitter. Take the first opportunity to humbly go to the other person and explain that you were hurt. You may find out that you misunderstood what happened, or that the other person just had a very difficult day. Perhaps they were wrong and need to apologize. Simply put, it is very important that you go back to the person that hurt you, because if you don't, bitterness can grow in *your* heart and that hurts *you* most of all. Cultivating a root of bitterness will inevitably lead to sin. In contrast to bitterness, think of the joy you will feel when the hurt feelings are resolved and your relationship is restored.

Conflict is normal in all relationships, so people must be able to disagree, yet disagree peacefully. Everyone needs to learn to meet conflicts head on and to seek the goal of understanding, resolution and restoration in relationships. Consider the following different ways to approach resolving a conflict:

❑ Mutually agree on a time to talk privately. Approach this time with a loving and caring attitude and without hostility.

❑ Stick to the issue at hand. Don't bring in other problems.

❑ Deal with the *issue*, do not attack the *person*.

❑ *Lower* your voice instead of raising it. Control your body and facial expressions.

❑ Express your own personal *feelings*. Use phrases such as, "I have a problem, I *feel* (sad, frustrated...) when this happens." This kind of comment can enlist their help. Avoid statements like, "You make me..." or "You always..." or "You never..." This only puts the other person on the defensive and creates more hard feelings.

❑ Don't withdraw into silence. This just leads to more frustration and anger.

❑ Seek to understand each other. Let the other person finish what he has to say without interrupting. When he is done, rephrase what you think the other person said and how you think he feels.

❏ If someone has a problem with something you did, listen carefully. He may have a good reason for feeling the way he does (we all have blind spots). You may need to seek forgiveness. If you feel you were not wrong, (without attacking or becoming overly defensive), gently explain your perspective in a humble way.

❏ Be willing to apologize sincerely when it is needed, and be willing to fully forgive without bearing a grudge. (Keep in mind that not every conflict must end up with one person being "right". There are times when it is okay to agree to disagree!)

❏ Discuss how the situation should have been handled differently. Give positive suggestions as to how a similar situation should be dealt with in the future. Resolve the current situation in a positive way that seeks mutual consideration of each individual involved.

❏ Restore the relationship. Shake hands or give a warm hug and reaffirm your love for the other person. Express words of encouragement and thank the other person for being willing to work through the conflict.

Remember: Conflict can be a positive force in bringing people closer together rather than pushing them further apart. It can bring deeper understanding of yourself and of the other people around you.

Parents: You may want to sit in as a silent observer or possible coach as you train your children through real life conflict resolution. Be careful not to allow the more verbally articulate child to manipulate the others.

❏ If you need help with solving a problem or you think someone may be in an unsafe situation, then it is appropriate to seek out a parent or other adult for help. Tattling, however, is reporting an incident to a parent or adult for the sole purpose of getting the other person in trouble. This is wrong and should not be done.

❏ All of us have sinned and offended not only God, but other people as well. Thankfully, we have received the grace and mercy of forgiveness from God as well as from others. When you have been forgiven, whether at a human level or from God above, gratefully accept that forgiveness in its fullness. Release the burden of guilt and live in the freedom and joy of forgiveness. God does not want us living under a weight of sin and guilt when He has so freely cleansed us from all our sin. (Of course, seek to not repeat the offense in the future.) (Matt. 18:21-22; Col. 3:13; 1 John 1:9)

FOR GENTLEMEN ONLY
Gentlemen can still show good manners toward women, no matter what the feminists say.

❑ Always hold a door open for a young girl or woman and wait for her to go through first. This includes opening and closing a lady's car door.

❑ Always seat ladies at the table first, and then take your seat.

❑ Rise from your seat when a lady enters a room and see that she has a comfortable place to sit.

❑ Help ladies with removing or putting on a sweater or coat.

❑ Remove your hat or cap when you go indoors. You should also remove your hat for prayer, the Pledge of Allegiance, the National Anthem, and for any other solemn occasion as a sign of respect.

❑ A gentleman always walks on the curbside of a sidewalk with a lady. (That way if a car comes along and splashes water and mud, he'll get wet and not her!)

❑ Always carry packages for a lady if you are walking together.

❑ When a female friend or associate needs to walk to a car in a darkened parking lot, it is polite and even chivalrous to offer to escort her in safety all the way to her vehicle. If you are dropping a lady off at her home or apartment, it is also polite to walk her to the front door. If she lives alone, remain long enough to see that all is secure inside before departing.

However, do not linger in a lady's apartment. That is inappropriate and will give the "appearance of evil." (1 Thess. 5:22)

❑ If a lady drops something, always stop and help her pick it up.

❑ Do not embarrass a lady by teasing, coarse jesting or belittling her in private or public. Always hold her up in honor. (Even if she is your sister!) (Eph. 4:29; 1 Pet. 3:10)

❑ Use self-control with your speech. Do not make off-color, or insinuating remarks or jokes to or about others. Let your speech always be filled with clean and wholesome conversation. See that in your words you reflect the purity of the Spirit of God that abides within you and for whom you are an ambassador. (Eph. 4:29; 5:4; 1 Tim. 4:12)

❑ Do not smoke, use drugs, abuse alcohol, or chew tobacco. Reject any offers made toward you to do so. As a true friend do not support or encourage these behaviors in others. A true friend would implore their friends to cease addictive and harmful activities. (Your body is the temple of the Holy Spirit. It is to be kept pure, holy, and controlled only by the Holy Spirit.) (1 Cor. 6:19-20; Eph 5:15-18)

❑ Do not make rude noises or laugh at others who behave inappropriately in public; this, of course, only encourages them to continue in their behavior. (Eph. 5:15-17)

❑ Do not do anything in dating or courtship that would violate or offend the purity of a young woman. Maintain purity in your thoughts, conversations, and actions. Uphold a lady's dignity and purity with respect and restraint. Flee situations that might lead to an opportunity for stumbling into sin. (1 Cor. 10:13; Eph. 5:1-7; 1 Thess. 4:1-8)

❑ Always treat Christian female friends as sisters and learn to develop healthy friendships. Encourage Christian sisters to a deeper walk, love and obedience to Christ. (Eph. 5:29; Heb. 3:13)

❑ Spend time with your parents discussing the differences between dating, courtship and their variations. Decide early on what would be the wisest course for you and why. Establish in your mind and heart firm physical and emotional boundaries in your relationships with young ladies before you get into situations you didn't expect or feel attractions that take you unaware.

❑ When thinking about marriage, consider what it is you are bringing to a marriage relationship:
- Are you loving unselfishly, seeking what is best for the other person?
- Have you prepared yourself for the real responsibilities of marriage?
- Have you sought to develop the spiritual and practical skills necessary to spiritually lead a family, take care of a home, provide financially, love unconditionally, and serve sacrificially – for better or worse, for richer or poorer, in sickness and in health?
- Have you sought permission to pursue a serious relationship from your parents and the parents of the young lady whom you believe God has brought into your life?
- Will you seek further counsel, permission and blessing from parents, and spiritual leaders in your life *before* engagement and marriage? (The best answer to the above questions should, of course, be "Yes.")

❑ God's desire is that you grow and mature into a godly man. Meditate upon God's Word in this regard and seek to fulfill this unique design given to you by your heavenly Father.

FOR LADIES ONLY
(Titus 2:3-5; 1 Peter 3:1-6)

❑ Accept all help graciously and politely.

❑ Do not play "feminist" if a male is gentlemanly.

❑ If a man does not offer to help you, do the task yourself without making him feel he is impolite.

❏ Keep your skirts down when playing or sitting. Cross your legs or ankles in a ladylike manner. Little girls should consider wearing shorts under a dress if playing on a playground.

❏ Dress and act modestly so others around you do not feel distracted or awkward.

❏ Be mindful of your tone of voice. Avoid being overly boisterous and loud. Pursue the *"unfading beauty of a gentle and quiet spirit, which is of great worth in God's sight."* 1 Peter 3:4 (1 Tim. 2:9-10; 1 Peter 1:13-16; 3:1-6)

❏ Do not embarrass a gentleman by teasing, coarse jesting or belittling him in private or public. Always hold him up in honor. (Even if he is your brother!) (Eph. 4:29; 1 Pet. 3:10)

❏ Use self-control with your speech. Do not make off-color, or insinuating remarks or jokes to or about others. Let your speech always be filled with clean and wholesome conversation. See that in your words you reflect the purity of the Spirit of God that abides within you and for whom you are an ambassador. (Eph. 4:29; 5:4; 1 Tim. 4:12)

❏ Do not smoke, use drugs, abuse alcohol, or chew tobacco. Reject any offers made toward you to do so. As a true friend do not support or encourage these behaviors in others. A true friend would implore their friends to cease addictive and harmful activities. (Your body is the temple of the Holy Spirit. It is to be kept pure, holy, and controlled only by the Holy Spirit.) (1 Cor. 6:19-20; Eph 5:15-18)

❏ Do not make rude noises or laugh at others who behave inappropriately in public; this, of course, only encourages them to continue in their behavior. (Eph. 5:15-17)

❏ Do not do anything in dating or courtship that would violate or offend the purity of a man. Maintain purity in your thoughts, conversations, and actions. Always uphold the dignity of a gentleman with respect and restraint. Be mindful not to allow or create an opportunity for stumbling into sin by the places you go, or the way you dress or behave. (1 Cor 10:13; Eph. 5:1-7; 1 Thess. 4:1-8)

❑ Always treat Christian gentlemen friends as brothers and learn to develop healthy friendships. Encourage Christian brothers to a deeper walk, love and obedience to Christ. (Eph. 5:29; Heb. 3:13)

❑ Spend time with your parents discussing the differences between dating, courtship and their variations. Decide early on what would be the wisest course for you and why. Establish in your mind and heart firm physical and emotional boundaries in your relationships with young men before you get into situations you didn't expect or feel attractions that take you unaware.

❑ When thinking about marriage, consider what it is you are bringing to a marriage relationship:
  • Are you loving unselfishly, seeking what is best for the other person?
  • Have you prepared yourself for the real responsibilities of marriage?
  • Have you sought to develop the spiritual and practical skills necessary to submit to the spiritual leadership of a husband, take care of a home, raise children, love unconditionally, and serve sacrificially – for better or worse, for richer or poorer, in sickness and in health?
  • Do you have the permission of your parents to enter into a more serious relationship with the young man whom you believe God has brought into your life?
  • Will you seek further counsel, permission and blessing from parents, and spiritual leaders in your life *before* engagement and marriage?
  (The best answer to the above questions should, of course, be "Yes.")

❑ God's desire is that you grow and mature into a godly woman. Meditate upon God's Word in this regard and seek to fulfill this unique design given to you by your heavenly Father.

SHOPPING

❑ Keep your hands to your self or in your pockets. Do not touch things in the store unless you are going to buy them. Learn to look with your eyes, not your fingers.

❑ Always stay with your parents in the store unless given permission otherwise.

❑ Use quiet "inside" voices in a store. Don't yell. (Prov. 25:28)

❑ Don't ever run in a store. You might knock something or someone else over, or even fall and get hurt yourself! (Prov. 25:28)

❑ If you knock something over and it breaks, let an employee know right away. Don't just walk away and leave it. (Prov. 28:13)

❑ When you push the cart, be careful that you don't bump into anyone. If you do bump into someone say, "Pardon me, I'm so sorry." Then be more careful! (Prov. 28:13)

❑ If there is a grocery cart traffic jam, be patient (with a smile), make room for others, and wait your turn. (Col. 3:12)

❑ Return your shopping cart to the storefront or the appropriate parking lot stall for carts.

❑ Do not ever, ever, steal! (Ex. 20:15; Eph. 4:28)

❑ If you are given too much change from the cashier, return the difference. If you keep it, it is a form of stealing. By returning it, you show your integrity and testimony as a Christian and thereby give glory to God.

❑ Be honest in all your business dealings. (Deut. 25:13-16; Prov. 11:1)

TRAVELING

❑   Always wear a seat belt.

❑   Never fight over who gets to sit where in a vehicle, whether it is a plane, train, car, bus, etc. You can discuss seating changes with another person, but it must be done in a courteous manner. (Parents: monthly seating charts can help to keep seating arrangements fair.) (Prov. 15:1; 17:14; 25:15)

❑   Do not try to change your seat after the car or bus is moving.

❑   If a woman or elderly person boards a crowded bus or subway, rise and give them your seat if no other seats are available. This is a polite and respectful thing to do. (Lev. 19:32)

❑   Be considerate of other passengers. If the bus is crowded, do not elbow or poke the person next to you. (Titus 3:2)

❑   Speak quietly and don't make loud noises in a car or bus so that you are not a distraction to the driver. (Prov. 25:28)

❑   If you get bored while traveling, don't grumble or complain. Quietly sing a song, listen to a story tape, or play a travel game. A cheerful passenger makes everyone's journey more pleasant. (Phil. 2:14)

❑   Do not make rude faces or gestures to other travelers or pedestrians.

❑   Don't ever stick a part of your body or an object out of a moving vehicle.

❑   Never throw objects or trash around *inside* a moving vehicle.

❑   Never throw any objects or trash *outside* of a moving vehicle. Keep it with you and put it in a proper receptacle when you arrive at your destination.

❑   Clean up your area of the car, bus, train or plane when you have reached your destination.

APPEARANCE
(1 Cor. 6:19)

❑ Issues of appearance and cleanliness deal with courtesy to others, especially when it involves your body and its proximity to others!

❑ Keep your teeth clean and breath fresh; brush at least twice a day and floss at least once daily.

❑ Bathe frequently, keep hair clean and well trimmed and watch body odor (use a deodorant). Be careful in your use of fragrance. Many people are sensitive to it so do not use too much.

❑ Keep your hair neatly trimmed and out of your eyes. Do not draw undue attention to yourself by outlandish hairstyles.

❑ Girls: Use make-up to enhance your natural beauty but do not let it become the focus of your appearance.

❑ Keep nails clean and trim.

❑ Do not pick at your skin, fingernails, scalp, ears, or nose in front of other people. Be careful where you scratch.

❑ Stand and sit straight (don't slump). Good posture will make you look and feel better.

❑ Maintain your proper weight through healthy eating and good exercise.

❑ Get plenty of rest so that you are bright-eyed and filled with energy. Do not stay up late reading or watching TV when you should be sleeping.

❑ Wear clean clothes in good repair.

❑ Learn to match colors and patterns of clothing. It can be fun to learn which colors and styles look best with your body shape, skin and hair color. This can help manage the size of your wardrobe and enable you to mix and match several outfits.

❑ Learn to select clothing that is appropriate for the occasion, such as: church, weddings, funerals, playing outside, gardening, painting, etc.

❑ Boys and girls need to be careful to wear modest clothing that is attractive, not inappropriately revealing or attracts undue attention. (1 Peter 1:13-16, 3:1-6)

❑ Compliment other people on their nice appearance, and if you receive a compliment always give a gracious "Thank you."

MEALTIMES
(1 Cor. 10:31)

❑ Learn how to properly set the table.

❑ When you come to the table, come with clean clothes, washed face and hands and combed hair.

❑ Get rid of chewing gum before you come to the table. Don't stick it on the side of your plate.

❑ Sit up straight with legs forward. Keep your legs to yourself so you don't kick the person across from you.

❑ Tipping a chair back on two legs risks injury to yourself and damage to the chair. Stay down on all four legs.

❑ Put the napkin in your lap just before you start to eat.

❑ Keep the hand you are not using in your lap.

❑ Be careful to keep your elbows off the table.

❑ Learn to use a knife and fork. When cutting meat, cut only 2 or 3 pieces at a time.

❑ Always be sure you take only your fair share of food and eat what you take. Do not always reach for what appears to be the biggest or the best piece. Do not eat more food than you need simply because it is available.

❑ Use only the serving spoon or fork to dish food onto your plate. Don't forget to put it back when you are done serving yourself.

❑ Wait for everyone else to receive their food at your table and for the hostess or host to take the first bite before you begin eating.

❑ If the meal is served in a formal manner, and you are unsure what to do, watch the host or hostess and follow their lead.

❑ If you need to go to the rest room while at the table, simply excuse yourself or say, "I'll be back in a moment."

❑ Talk in "indoor" voices at the table and take care not to dominate the conversation. Listen to what others have to share. (Prov. 18:13)

❑ Don't play with your food. If it is not real "finger food" then your fingers should not touch it.

❑ Bring your food to your mouth and bend slightly over your plate. Don't hunker down and start shoveling it in like a human backhoe.

❑ You may use a knife or a piece of bread to help push the last bits of food onto your fork, but never use your fingers.

❑ Eat neatly and periodically dab at your lips and corners of your mouth with your napkin. Dab at your mouth before drinking from a water goblet to avoid leaving greasy lip marks on the rim of your glass.

❑ Try not to make a mess around your plate or on the floor. If you accidentally spill, apologize and clean it up yourself. Pick up anything you drop.

❑ Never reach across someone else's plate to get something. Say, "Mom, would you please pass the butter?" And when you receive it, say, "Thank you." Then Mom can say, "You're welcome!"

❑ Don't over-fill your mouth till you have "chipmunk cheeks". Take smaller bites.

❑ If you find a bone, pit or seed in your mouth, remove it from your mouth with a spoon or your fingers and set it on the side of your plate. If you can't swallow what is in your mouth due to any other reason, quietly expel it from your mouth into your napkin. (If you are choking, grab your throat and let the person next to you be aware of your problem. Be familiar with the Heimlich maneuver so you can come to the aid of others.)

❑ Do not be a picky eater. Eat a little of everything that is served. If you don't care for it, leave the rest on your plate without any comments. Never say to a cook, "I don't like that," or "I can't eat that." It is most unmannerly!

❑ Eat quietly, don't slurp or smack. Chew your food with your lips together.

❑ Don't speak with food in your mouth. Wait to speak until after you swallow!

❑ If you must burp, do it as quietly as possible, and then say, "Excuse me."

❑ Whether you are at home or a guest at someone else's house, always express sincere appreciation to the cook. They have spent considerable time preparing a meal for you to enjoy.

❑ When you are finished eating, lay your knife and fork across your plate. If your napkin is a paper one, leave it on the table beside your plate. If it is a cloth napkin, fold it and set it beside your plate, or put it back in the napkin ring.

❑ You may ask to be excused from the table when home, but not when you are a guest at someone else's table. You may be excused as a guest when the host or hostess rises and invites you to leave the table or when their children are excused.

❑ Always clear away your own plate. Do not leave it for others to clean up after you, unless you are dining formally and are being waited on.

❑ In your own home, always help with the dishes after a meal unless excused by a parent. When you are a guest, always rise and offer to help with the dishes.

AT CHURCH

❑ Enter a church service reverently. If it is acceptable to speak to those around you, do so in a quiet voice so as not to disturb those who may be praying or preparing their hearts for worship.

❑ Be sure to visit the restroom and get a drink before a church service begins. It is very distracting to the person preaching as well as to the congregation for people to be going in and out of the sanctuary for these reasons.

❑ Be courteous and friendly. If you see that someone needs a place to sit, move over to make room for them. If they are visitors, be sure to welcome them. Introduce yourself, and let them know how glad you are that they came to church or Sunday School.

❑ Learn to follow along in a church service. Stand when others stand, sing when they sing, pray when they pray. Seek to focus your thoughts on the sermon. Find ways to apply what you have learned to your daily life.

❑ When you are in church, sit still and do not talk or make noise. It will cause a distraction for those around you and make it difficult for them to listen. If you are still very young and allowed to have a notepad or Bible coloring book in church, use them *very quietly* and only after singing time is over and the adult teaching time has begun.

❏ As you get older, learn how to take notes. This can begin by keeping a tally of every time you hear the word "God," "Jesus," "love," etc. As you get older, copy your parent's notes. Before you know it you will be listening for yourselves and keeping notes on your own!

❏ If you must chew gum, do it with your mouth closed and without snapping or blowing bubbles (this is true in other public places as well). Chew softly instead of vigorously chomping away. Consider quietly sucking on a mint or fruit flavored hard candy instead.

❏ Don't shove to the front of the line when at a church potluck. Wait patiently and don't overfill your plate. Remember that people are more important than food. Make sure there is plenty left for others who will come behind you. (Phil. 2:3)

❏ Don't run or play roughly inside the church or on the patio areas. The elderly or parents with babies and toddlers can be bumped and get hurt.

❏ If you are outside the sanctuary during church services or Sunday school (such as when you arrive late), walk and talk quietly so that you are not heard inside the building.

❏ Show respect for the church sanctuary even when church is over. Do not run, make loud noises, climb on the platform area or play with the musical instruments or sound equipment.

❏ Protect and help take care of your church property. Do not damage or write on any furniture, equipment or buildings. Do not leave litter lying around. Even if someone else dropped it, pick it up and throw it away. Do whatever you can to have your church be a place where visitors will be happy to come.

MISCELLANEOUS MOMENTS
(Prov. 20:11; Matt. 7:12; 1 Cor. 10:31-33; Phil. 2:3)

❑ Always turn your head and cover your mouth whenever you cough or sneeze. Wash your hands at the first opportunity.

❑ If your nose is running, excuse yourself and privately blow it into a tissue or handkerchief. Don't sniff! Keep a clean handkerchief or tissues with you.

❑ If you belch say, "Excuse me." (If other gases seek to escape, excuse yourself, and find a bathroom.)

❑ Do not spit in public.

❑ When you yawn, do so quietly and cover your mouth. Then say, "Excuse me."

❑ When at a public place such as school, church or other gathering, be courteous and friendly. Reach out to those who may be new and introduce them to others.

❑ Show respect and good stewardship toward your own as well as other people's property.

❑ If you are at a concert, play, or movie, sit still and do not talk until the intermission. It will distract others and hinder their enjoyment.

❑ If you are sent an invitation that asks for a response (RSVP), be sure to respond by phone or letter promptly.

❑ Whenever someone does something nice for you, invites you to a special event, or gives you a gift, be sure to let them know how thankful you are. Write them a thank-you letter as soon as you can!

❑ Learn how to hold a baby and be gentle.

❑ Be kind and gentle to your animals and pets. (Prov. 12:10a)

❑ When in a waiting room, such as at a doctor's office, sit and read or talk quietly. Do not run around or make loud noises. If a play area is available, play quietly.

❑ Be respectfully quiet when you are in a library. Other people are trying to read.

❑ There are times when you *must* use bad manners and be rude when you are without a responsible adult. Do not ever speak to strangers, go anywhere with them or get into their car, no matter how nice they are or what they say. If they try to make you, kick and scream. Yell loudly, "You're not my mom (or dad)!!" And do your best to run away.

❑ Live each day knowing that Jesus is with you, watching each action, knowing each thought, and hearing each spoken word. Seek to bring Him glory in all that you do.

For the Grace of God that brings salvation has appeared to all men. It teaches us to say "No" to ungodliness and worldly passions, and to live self-controlled, upright and godly lives in this present age, while we wait for the blessed hope – the glorious appearing of our great God and Savior, Jesus Christ, who gave himself for us to redeem us from all wickedness and to purify for himself a people that are his very own, eager to do what is good. Titus 2:11-14

May our homes reflect all the goodness and love of the Lord.
May we shine as a gracious beacon of light
to those who are around us
so that the name of our
Father in Heaven
is lifted up in praise.

Chapter Six

Practical Living
Skills

⚜

T here are many skills that both boys and girls should be prepared to
do before they leave the home. These include practical skills that
relate to areas within, as well as without, the household. It is common
to think of skills as being stereotypically divided into male and female tasks,
however, no parent knows what the Lord has in mind for their children.
Therefore, it is wise to train both boys and girls in every area of life – inside
and outside jobs, cooking, cleaning, mowing, simple automotive repairs, etc.

The following list includes many of these skills. This list has been divided
into generalized age categories for your convenience and to help you space out
the training of new skills. Please let this list be a simple guide to prompt your
thinking; a tool in your hands, not your master. These are only *suggested ages*
as to when you may wish to begin introducing various skills – *not an inflexible
list of tasks locked into a specific age.* There may be skills presented that do not
apply to your own family's personality (i.e. hunting skills). There may also be
skills that you, the parent, do not have but that you want to develop in your
children. In these instances, perhaps there is a friend, family member or a class
where they can be taught. You may even want to learn together. There may be
skills that you present earlier than listed and some that you present much later
due to the uniqueness of each of your children and your lifestyle. Enjoy that
uniqueness and let your children's abilities help set the pace.

Any new skill will of course bring a challenge to them, but if it is in the
realm of their abilities, then all they will need is your patient teaching and lots
of encouragement. Remember, the goal is to have children proficient in practical living skills so that they can become responsible adults, equipped to minister in the lives of their own family as well as in the lives of others.

During the training process it is essential that you maintain a positive
environment. Despite notions to the contrary, expressing praise does not come

naturally to most people. It is something that each person must purpose to do in his or her own heart and mind. Remember, all children need honest praise and encouraging words. *Look for opportunities where they have done something well with a right heart and praise them for it.* It is unlikely that young children will perform all their tasks with the same expertise that you do. Be patient. Give them time, some encouragement, and someday you will find that they will do the job as well or better than you ever did.

Recognition of their progress in positive behaviors goes a very long way to insure that the right attitudes and right actions will continue. Be careful not to always sandwich your compliments with criticism, correction or ideas for improvement. It can be demotivating to hear, "You have done a nice job, *but...*" This is especially true when they have worked hard and feel that they have done their best. Save those comments for another time. When the job needs to be repeated, that can be the time to teach them what can be done to improve their work. Let your children drink from the refreshing cup of your pure encouragement and praise.

In addition to the skills list are some helpful hints and charts that can assist you in the training process. Some of the jobs, as you will see, are those that are done routinely. Other jobs are those that are done infrequently, such as during "spring-cleaning". As you train your children in different skills, the tasks they learn will often become their regular "chores." Help your children see that chores are not punitive! Chores are tasks that are shared by mutually responsible members of a family that work together as well as play together. Everyone is on the same team. Each person is playing a vital part in making the home a place of beauty, comfort, and loving refuge.

HELPFUL HINTS FOR DILIGENT KIDS

- Don't expect young children to do a task all alone the first time. Work alongside them until they understand what to do and how to do it themselves.

- Keep the job simple enough for the child's age and ability.

- Take the time to teach your children *how* to do the job.

- Don't do anything for your children that they can do for themselves.

- If a mess is very large, children may feel overwhelmed and will need your help. To help them avoid large messes, limit the number of available toys by using a toy rotation system. In addition, teach them to put one toy away before taking out another one.

- Teach them efficient work skills so they don't waste time or energy unnecessarily (i.e. teach them to work clockwise around the room.) Have them carry a basket to hold items that need to be put away.

- Beds for younger children can be made easier if you eliminate a top sheet and use a comforter, or a sleeping bag. Then all they need to do is smooth it out and put their pillow on top.

- Bedrooms can be picked up easier if there are shelves and baskets for storing toys and special treasures. ("A place for everything and everything in its place.")

- Younger children can hang up their own clothes if you lower the rod for them in their closet. To do this inexpensively, hang a broom handle from the upper rod in the closet by attaching ropes or chains on each end.

- Keep a bucket or "carry-all" with all the necessary cleaning supplies under the bathroom sink. It makes the cleaning job much easier for everyone. (If little ones are around, you may want to use a cupboard safety latch to protect them from dangerous chemicals.)

- Use job charts such as "My Helping Hand" (page 116) for daily chores, or create your own job lists. Charts and lists can help children remember what they need to do and pace their work.

- Be careful not to add on more jobs if the original list is accomplished.

- Give a variety of jobs and rotate them regularly so everybody learns the necessary skills.

- If you have a "work day" set aside, let them know about it ahead of time. Plan breaks for snack and play time. Splurge and have a pizza dinner when all the work is done!

- Put reminder posters or cards in each room with a checklist describing what needs to be done for the job to be done right. For example:

BEDROOM	
• Bed made	• Drawers and closet door closed
• Under bed clean	• Floor picked up
• Drawers neat	• Night stand, desk, and shelves
• Closet clothes hanging straight	clean and neat
	• Surfaces dusted
• Closet floor straightened	• Floors vacuumed

- Use consequences when necessary for wrong attitudes, poor or neglected work. A natural consequence for work habitually left undone would be that a job not done would cost one more job to pay for it.

- Use a "Diligent Kids" chart (page 117) or any other kind of achievement chart of your own. Establish predetermined privileges that can be earned as they learn new jobs or skills, or become accustomed to new routines, etc. These privileges can be outings, books, games, money, or anything else enjoyable. This provides excitement and motivation!

- Praise your children for great attitudes and jobs well done. Give them a special treat when they least expect it!

Colossians 3:17: *And whatever you do, whether in word or deed, do it all in the name of the Lord Jesus, giving thanks to God the Father through Him.*

Colossians 3:23: *Whatever you do, work at it with all your heart, as working for the Lord, not for men.*

PRACTICAL LIVING SKILLS CHECKLIST

Remember: These are merely *suggested* ages when you may wish to introduce a new skill. Mastery of any skill will come at different times for different children. Endeavor to work alongside your child as you begin to introduce new skills – remembering that training takes patience and learning takes time and repetition. Seek to provide an enthusiastic environment so that developing new skills is a delightful experience for all!

Write the child's name or initials under the "name" heading. As you teach the skills listed, either check off or date their box when they have come to an understanding of how that job is to be performed.

Practical Living Skills AGE 2	Name	Name	Name	Name
Undress self				
Put own pajamas away				
Wash face and hands				
Comb or brush own hair (with help)				
Brush teeth (with help)				
Pick up toys (with help)				
Tidy up bedroom (with help)				
Clear off own place at table				
Be able to play safely and alone with selected toys for a set period of time (1/2 to 1 hr.) in own room. (This is still under supervision. Children need to know that they can be alone, and still have fun. They do not always need to be entertained.)				

AGE 3	Name	Name	Name	Name
Dress self (with help)				
Put dirty clothes in hamper				
Make own bed (pull up comforter, straighten pillow and top with stuffed toy)				
Wipe up own spills				
Help set table				
Help clear table				
Snap, zipper, and button				
AGE 4				
Introduce "My Helping Hand" to help remind your child to perform their personal responsibilities every day (page 116)				
Help gather laundry				
Pick up toys and tidy bedroom routinely				
Pick up outside toys in the yard				
Shake out area rugs				
Dust and clean TV screen				
Empty wastebaskets				
Memorize own phone number (learn it to a melody!)				
Help empty dishwasher				
Help bring in groceries				
Tie own shoes				
Sit quietly in church (looking at books or drawing quietly is okay)				

AGE 5	Name	Name	Name	Name
Put clean clothes away neatly				
Clean own fingernails				
Leave bathroom clean and tidy after use				
Clean toilet				
Clean brushes and combs				
Organize bathroom drawers				
Feed and water pets				
Get mail (if supervised) and put it in the proper place				
Memorize own address (sing to a new melody!)				
Begin to understand the differences and value of money				
Receive a small allowance (if used)				
Begin learning about saving, spending and giving				
Know how to make an emergency phone call (911)				
Dust low shelves and objects (consider using a feather duster)				
Empty kitchen trash				
Pour milk into cereal				
Pour milk or juice into a cup				
Learn to roller skate				
Learn to jump rope				
Begin learning how to swim				

AGE 6	Name	Name	Name	Name
Keep dresser drawers neat and tidy				
Keep closet neat and tidy				
Empty dishwasher and put dishes away				
Set and clear table				
Wash and dry dishes by hand				
Help put groceries away				
Make juice from a can of frozen concentrate				
Make sandwiches				
Make toast				
Help make gelatin desserts or instant pudding				
Wash out plastic trash cans				
Clean mirrors				
Bathe alone				
Spot clean walls and switch plates				
Straighten living and family room				
Rake leaves				
Bring in firewood				
Begin sewing easy pictures, i.e. Plastic canvas				
Build a beginner snap-together car model following the directions				

AGE 7	Name	Name	Name	Name
Clean pet cages and food bowls				
Use a vacuum cleaner				
Use a broom and dustpan				
Sweep floors, porches, decks, driveways, garage and walkways				
Take a written phone message				
Learn basic food groups and good nutrition habits				
Cook canned soup				
Read and follow a simple recipe				
Measure with cooking tools properly				
Make gelatin desserts or puddings alone				
Pack own sack lunch				
Boil eggs (hard and soft)				
Cut up own meat, pancakes, etc.				
Water outside plants, flowers and garden				
Weed flower beds and vegetable garden				
Chop kindling				
Strip bed sheets				
Carry dirty clothes hamper to laundry room				
Sort clothes for washing by color and fabric and check pockets				
Straighten book and toy shelves				
Begin music lessons				
Encourage a beginning reader to read the Bible. (A beginner Bible would be a great gift)				

AGE 8	Name	Name	Name	Name
Read the Bible and pray everyday				
Fold clothes neatly without wrinkles				
Hang clothes on line for sun drying				
Iron flat items				
Remake own bed with clean sheets				
Polish own shoes				
Clean interior of car				
Vacuum furniture (i.e., chairs and couches), especially under cushions				
Water house plants				
Water lawn outside				
Clean bathroom sink, toilet and tub				
Wash and dry dishes by hand or load and turn on dishwasher				
Mop floors				
Peel carrots and potatoes				
Clean and trim own finger and toe nails				
Build more complicated models of cars, boats or airplanes				
String fishing line on a fishing pole				
Learn more hand sewing such as simple decorative embroidery or crewel work				

AGE 9	Name	Name	Name	Name
Read the Bible and pray everyday				
Load and operate washing machine				
Load and operate dryer				
Clean lint trap and washer filter				
Fold sheets and blankets neatly				
Straighten and organize kitchen drawers				
Help clean out refrigerator				
Prepare hot beverages				
Prepare boxed macaroni and cheese				
Cook hot dogs				
Cook eggs: scrambled, fried, boiled, poached, and omelets				
Brown hamburger meat				
Dust all household furniture				
Count and give monetary change				
Compare quality and prices (unit pricing)				
Begin learning basic carpentry, i.e. build a bird house from a kit				
Begin learning needlework such as crochet and knitting				
Maintain bicycle by regular cleaning, and oiling				

AGE 10	Name	Name	Name	Name
Read the Bible and pray everyday				
Replace light bulbs and understand wattage				
Clean fireplace/woodstove				
Wipe down kitchen cupboards				
Be able to do family laundry completely				
Polish furniture				
Distinguish between good and spoiled food				
Bake a cake from a mix				
Bake cookies from scratch				
Cook frozen and canned vegetables				
Make pancakes from scratch				
Understand the importance of ingredient and nutrient labeling				
Plan a balanced meal				
Learn simple first aid for minor cuts and bruises				
Understand uses of medicine and seriousness of overuse				
Repair bicycle tire and learn basic adjustments				
Mow lawn				
Know how to handle a pocketknife				
Sew simple crafts on a sewing machine (pillows, bean bags etc.)				

AGE 11	Name	Name	Name	Name
Read the Bible and pray everyday				
Polish silver, copper, and brass				
Replace fuse or know where house breakers are				
Change vacuum belt and bag				
Clean and straighten garage				
Bake muffins and biscuits				
Make a green salad and salad dressing				
Do simple mending such as sewing on buttons and fixing hems				
Wash the car				
Learn proper safety and handling of machinery to which they have access (with supervision!)				
Do a complete job of lawn maintenance: mowing, edging, raking, sweeping, etc.				
Learn how to tie a variety of knots				
Understand basics of photography				
Be a helper in a church ministry (i.e. Nursery, Sunday School, gardening)				

AGE 12	Name	Name	Name	Name
Read the Bible and pray everyday (without being reminded)				
Parents: you can begin providing more Bible study materials, Christian biographies and devotionals to build up their library				
Select/purchase own personal hygiene supplies (i.e. deodorant, hair goods, etc.)				
Tie a neck-tie (boys and girls)				
Know methods of basic spot removal for oil, blood, coffee, tea, soda, fruit etc. (keep a chart handy)				
Iron all types of clothing				
Hand wash delicates or woolens				
Begin sewing simple clothing on sewing machine				
Prepare hamburgers				
Make spaghetti				
Bake bread				
Organize pantry				
Clean refrigerator				
Clean stove and oven interior and exterior				
Clean tubs, shower stall walls and shower curtains				
Build fire in fireplace				
Build fire in campfire				
Set up a tent				

AGE 13	Name	Name	Name	Name
Read the Bible and pray everyday				
Take ownership of personal grooming. Arrange with parent for haircuts, clothing needs, etc.				
Learn how to select and prepare fruits and vegetables				
Prepare simple dinners				
Go clothes shopping in several stores. Compare prices and selection between thrift stores, outlet stores and regular department stores.				
Establish a savings account				
Make deposits and withdrawals at bank and automated teller machine				
Establish and use a simple budget; keep records in a ledger or on the computer				
Learn how to place a long distance call				
Learn how to place a collect call				
Help paint a room				
Oil squeaks in chairs, doors or hinges				
Help clean and organize garage, storage closets and attic space				
Wash windows and screens inside and out				
Clean and oil window tracks				
Unplug a sink or toilet with a plunger or chemicals				

AGE 13 (continued)	Name	Name	Name	Name
Chop and stack firewood				
Produce a usable product from wood, such as a shelf or small table				
Go hunting with an experienced parent or other adult and learn proper safety guidelines				
Take First Aid, CPR, and baby-sitting certification courses				

AGE 14	Name	Name	Name	Name
Read the Bible and pray everyday				
Scrub down walls				
Strip and wax floors				
Clean bathroom tile and grout				
Install doorknobs and locks				
Change plug on electric cord				
Rewire a lamp				
Change furnace or AC filters				
Properly return items to a store				
Repot or transplant plants				
Fertilize lawn				
Polish car				
Repair fences, outbuildings or barns				
Know the differences between appearance, usage, and clean-up of various paints, stains and lacquers				
Help paint exterior of house				
Clean eaves and gutters				
Be familiar with computers				
Type with proficiency				
Read a bus schedule and plan a short trip around town				
Help plan, prepare and set up for a camping trip				

AGE 15	Name	Name	Name	Name
Read the Bible and pray everyday				
Plan and shop for three days of meals (with parent)				
Prepare more complex meals				
Fry, roast and bake chicken				
Stuff and roast a turkey				
Roast a roast				
Carve meat such as turkey or roasts and section a chicken				
Make homemade soups and stews				
Help plan, prepare soil and plant a vegetable garden				
Learn pruning methods for trees and shrubs				
Know how to freeze and can fruits and vegetables				
Know how to make jams and jellies				
Know how to dry foods				
Understand causes and prevention of food poisoning				
Defrost refrigerator and freezer				
Maintain a personal organizer				
Fill car with gas				
Check and fill all car fluids – brake, transmission, motor oil, radiator antifreeze, and windshield solution; fill tires with air				
Replace faucet washer				
Repair/replace a screen				
Help hang wallpaper				
Understand basic electronics to do simple repairs				

AGE 16 and up	Name	Name	Name	Name
Read the Bible and pray everyday				
Be able to clearly communicate the gospel of Jesus Christ and how to receive His gift of salvation				
Be able to share a personal testimony of God's redeeming work in your life				
Prepare full, balanced meals completely, from planning to shopping to preparation				
Do more difficult sewing, mending and complex needlework				
Learn basics of interior design				
Learn to give simple haircuts and trims				
Take clothes in for dry cleaning and pick up when finished				
Steam clean or shampoo carpets and upholstery				
Weather-strip and caulk around doors and windows				
Replace kitchen and bathroom grout or sealant				
Learn basics of indoor and outdoor plumbing				
Repair small holes in walls with putty				
Obtain a drivers license and drive a car wisely, lawfully and carefully				
Learn basics of automotive care: tune-ups, oil changes, tire changes, brakes, repairs, maintenance, etc.				

AGE 16 and up (continued)	Name	Name	Name	Name
Maintain records of car repairs and routine maintenance				
Establish a checking account				
Write checks and balance checkbook				
Have solid understanding of personal financial responsibility (know how to handle money wisely and keep records)				
Fill out a job application				
Type a resume				
Know what to look for in purchasing or renting a house or apartment				
Know how to arrange for the standard set up of household services such as power, gas, phone, water and trash removal				
Understand what household bills must be paid and when, i.e. Rent, mortgage, phone, power, water, garbage, etc.				
Understand various types of insurance, and compare coverages				
Fill out income tax forms				
Be familiar with city, state and federal taxes (especially for when you are a home owner or become self-employed)				
Understand local government and community resources				
Understand the differences in political parties and formulate your own opinion				

AGE 16 and up (continued)	Name	Name	Name	Name
Register to vote (age 18)				
Young men register for the draft (age 18) as required by law				
Obtain high school diploma or GED				
Continue preparation for the future with vocational training, apprenticeship or further college education				
Determine from Scripture what qualifications are given for a godly spouse; determine first to *become* a godly partner before you seek to find one				

There will always be more that you may want to add to this list. However, if this much is accomplished before your children leave home, you can feel that you have done a great job in preparing them for their future!

My Helping Hand

Comb my hair

Do my Special Jobs

Brush my teeth

Wash my face

Make my bed and get dressed

DILIGENT KIDS GOLD STAR CHART

NAME	NAME	NAME	NAME
GOLD STARS	GOLD STARS	GOLD STARS	GOLD STARS
CHORES Get dressed, make bed, tidy room, wash face, brush teeth, comb hair SPECIAL JOBS	CHORES Get dressed, make bed, tidy room, wash face, brush teeth, comb hair SPECIAL JOBS	CHORES Get dressed, make bed, tidy room, wash face, brush teeth, comb hair SPECIAL JOBS	CHORES Get dressed, make bed, tidy room, wash face, brush teeth, comb hair SPECIAL JOBS

Accomplishing the items on the above list with a good attitude and without being reminded, will earn one gold star! As the stars accumulate you can earn the following:

25 STARS EARNS:_____   75 STARS EARNS: _____

50 STARS EARNS:_____   100 STARS EARNS: _____

Chapter Seven

Personal Safety

D o this, don't do that ... do it this way, don't do it that way ...
Sometimes it can seem like there is no end to the rules that children
must be told. However, when you pause to think about it, many of
the guidelines you teach are for their personal protection. As parents you simply want them to avoid any unnecessary pain and injury. If your children can
understand that many of these guidelines are for their safety, then learning
them won't seem like just a list of "do's and don'ts." As a result, obeying them
will be easier because they will understand the "why" behind the guideline.

Knowledge, understanding and wisdom go hand in hand. And in the area
of personal safety, parents want to make sure that their children are sufficiently
wise and capable of applying what they have been taught. Therefore, begin by
instructing with the following verses from God's Word, the source of wisdom.
Instill in your children an unwavering confidence of their security in the
good hand of God. Teach them that they are never alone, no matter what the
circumstances of life may bring. Even though sad things happen in our
lives, God sees a far greater picture than we are able to. The glorious out-
come of every facet of our lives, the good and seemingly bad, are all in His
sovereign hand.

*Remember: These guidelines are listed only as references for you to use in help-
ing your children protect themselves.* There are other safety precautions that wise
parents will make to provide a safe environment in their homes, but these are
not included here. As you go through this section, please remember to share
only those guidelines that you believe are applicable to your children. Take
time to discuss what you want your children to understand. You may not need
to teach them every single guideline here.

The following safety guidelines are divided into several different categories. They are:

- Safety From God's Word
- Safety Guidelines
- General Principles
- Swimming
- Hiking
- Playgrounds
- Pedestrians
- Bikes
- Motor Vehicles
- Sharp and Dangerous Things
- Electricity
- Hot Stuff
- Fire
- Animals
- Strangers
- Touching

SAFETY FROM GOD'S WORD

Psalm 121: *I will lift up my eyes to the hills – where does my help come from? My help comes from the Lord, the Maker of heaven and earth. He will not let your foot slip – He who watches over you will not slumber; indeed, He who watches over Israel will neither slumber nor sleep. The Lord watches over you – the Lord is your shade at your right hand; the sun will not harm you by day, nor the moon by night. The Lord will keep you from all harm – He will watch over your life; the Lord will watch over your coming and going both now and forevermore.*

Psalm 4:8: *I will lie down and sleep in peace, for you alone, O Lord, make me dwell in safety.*

Psalm 16:1: *Keep me safe, O God, for in you I take refuge.*

Psalm 27:1: *The Lord is my light and my salvation – whom shall I fear? The Lord is the stronghold of my life – of whom shall I be afraid?*

Psalm 56:3-4: *When I am afraid, I will trust in you. In God, whose word I praise, in God I trust; I will not be afraid. What can mortal man do to me?*

Psalm 91:1-2: *He who dwells in the shelter of the Most High will rest in the shadow of the Almighty. I will say of the Lord, "He is my refuge and my fortress, my God, in whom I trust."*

Proverbs 1:33: *...but whoever listens to me will live in safety and be at ease, without fear of harm.*

Proverbs 3:21-24: *My son, preserve sound judgment and discernment, do not let them out of your sight; they will be life for you, an ornament to grace your neck. Then you will go on your way in safety, and your foot will not stumble; when you lie down, you will not be afraid; when you lie down, your sleep will be sweet.*

Proverbs 14:26: *He who fears the Lord has a secure fortress, and for his children it will be a refuge.*

Proverbs 28:26: *He who trusts in himself is a fool, but he who walks in wisdom is kept safe.*

Proverbs 29:25: *Fear of man will prove to be a snare, but whoever trusts in the Lord is kept safe.*

Isaiah 41:10: *So do not fear, for I am with you; do not be dismayed, for I am your God. I will strengthen you and help you; I will uphold you with my righteous right hand.*

SAFETY GUIDELINES
The following guidelines will help you as a parent take advantage of teaching/training opportunities with your children.

General Principles

❑ Wear shoes outside.

❑ Keep your shoelaces tied.

❑ Use handrails when going up or down stairs. Do not run down stairs.

❑ Keep toys away from the top and bottom of stairs (and anywhere in between).

❑ Do not climb into trunks or old refrigerators. You may get locked in and have little or no air to breathe.

❑ Never stand up in a grocery cart; you could flip out onto your head.

❑ Do not climb in a grocery cart unassisted; you could tip the cart over on top of you.

❑ Keep fingers, hands and toes away from the wheels of grocery carts.

❑ When shopping, keep your arms to your sides so you don't bump anything. You don't want to break glass or cause slippery liquids to fall on the floor.

❑ Keep little "things" (toys, pins or needles for sewing, pencils, pens, money, etc.) out of your mouth. Help keep small items, such as these, away from babies and toddlers.

❑ Don't eat any berries or leaves off of a plant until an adult has confirmed their safety.

❑ Do not touch or swallow any unknown liquids, powders or medicines in your house or anywhere else. (All cleaning chemicals and **medi**cines should be up high where little ones cannot get them.)

❑ Do not take any medicine unless a parent (or other authorized adult) gives it to you.

❑ Always say "NO" to smoking, drugs, and alcohol. What may seem "momentarily' cool is a one-way road to long-term pain, disappointment and personal destruction.

❑ Do not run with sharp objects (sticks, pencils, knives, screwdrivers, etc.) in your hands.

❑ Do not run or play with toys, sticks, toothbrushes, suckers, etc., in your mouth.

❑ Do not run or make jokes with food in your mouth; you could easily choke.

❑ Never play with or around an opening or closing garage door. It is not a toy. If it is automatic, make sure no one is near when opening or closing the door.

❑ Never stand on the very top rung of a ladder.

❑ When you lift a heavy object, don't bend from the waist. Bend your knees and squat with your back straight. Get a good grip before you pick it up, and hold it close to your body.

❑ Don't be rough with children who are younger then you are. Adapt your level of play when you are with children who are smaller than you.

❑ Learn how to handle babies gently and securely.

❑ Learn how to dress appropriately for the weather. It is always wise to have a jacket handy when you leave home. If it is not needed it can always be left in the car.

❑ Protect yourself from the sun – use hats and sunscreen. Stay in shady areas when it is excessively hot to prevent sunstroke. Drink plenty of fluids.

❑ Remember that you can get a serious sunburn even on cloudy days.

❑ Be careful when playing with ropes. They can be fun to use for pulleys, jumping, etc., but they can be dangerous, too. Do not tie up a person with ropes when playing.

❑ Be a good steward of your own personal health.

❑ Dress warmly when needed.

❑ Avoid sharing someone else's comb or brush.

❑ Use only your own toothbrush. Keep it from touching others.

❑ Use only your own drinking cup, plate and silverware at the table.

❑ Wash your hands frequently in soap and water – especially when:
  • You have used the restroom
  • You have been out in public
  • You have cared for someone who is sick
  • You will be preparing food
  • You have worked in the dirt
  • You are going to eat

❑ Cover public toilet seats.

❑ When you are ill, receive the proper rest and/or medication as needed.

❑ Maintain good habits regarding proper nutrition, exercise, and sleep.

❑ Don't play in or around dumps or junkyards, on railroad property or tracks, empty houses, houses under construction, irrigation ditches, mining holes, shafts or wells.

❑ Never give or accept a "dare" from anyone. This is fools territory. Do not attempt to do something which makes you very afraid or very uncomfortable simply because your courage is being challenged. Never challenge someone else's courage in a potentially dangerous activity.

❑ During a lightening storm, do not go under trees, or stay in or near water (pools, hot tubs or even the bathtub). Do not stand by windows, sink faucets, fireplaces or radiators. Do not use the telephone. Unplug your TV and computer. All these items attract and conduct electricity.

❏ During an earthquake, go under a solid piece of furniture or under a doorway. Watch for falling objects or structural materials. If outside, stay in an open area away from any objects that could fall on you.

❏ During tornadoes, seek out a basement or an underground storm cellar. If these are not available get under a sturdy table or workbench, or get in the smallest room with the strongest walls. Do not stay in a car, trailer or mobile home. If caught near a ditch lie down in it and shield your head. Cover your face with clothing to keep out the dust. Get out of large open buildings like theaters and gymnasiums.

❏ If warned of an approaching hurricane, evacuate the area. Do not stay in a structure that is not sturdy such as a trailer or mobile home. Turn off electricity, gas and water and then leave. If caught in a storm, go to a small interior room in the house with sturdy walls and shut the door. If the storm dies suddenly, stay inside. Open the windows on the opposite side of the building because the center of the storm is passing and the wind will resume from the opposite direction. Afterward, watch out for downed power lines and debris.

❏ In the event of a flash flood, do not try to save anything. Leave immediately. If caught in the flood, always seek higher ground. Watch for rock and mud slides and fallen power lines. Do not drive through floodwater.

❏ Be equipped for natural disasters. Prepare a Disaster Supplies Kit. The following items might be included:
  • Supply of water (one gallon per person per day for about 3 days). Store water in sealed, unbreakable containers. Replace every six months.
  • Water purification tablets
  • High energy foods – granola bars, trail mix, jerky, dehydrated foods
  • Extra clothing
  • Blankets or sleeping bags
  • First aid kit and prescription medicine
  • Battery powered radio, flashlight and plenty of extra batteries, glow sticks
  • Extra set of car keys

- List of family doctors, medical history and important family information
- Deck of cards, small games, coloring books and crayons, paper, pens and pencils
- For more ideas and supplies, contact your local American Red Cross

The wise parent will teach their children how to:

❑ In the event of a natural disaster, know how to turn off electricity, gas and water from their main switches. Do not drink water until you are sure of its purity. Stay calm and keep together. Listen to the radio and follow the directions that are given.

❑ When age appropriate, teach your children how and when to make an emergency phone call (911). If they need to dial 911, they should tell the operator their name, always speaking loudly, slowly and clearly. They should calmly follow directions and stay on the phone.

❑ Learn your family's home address and telephone number and know how to contact your parents or a trusted adult if there is an emergency. In addition, know your parent's or a close relative's work telephone number.

❑ Have a family code word, so that if your parents ever need to have trusted adults contact you, they will have been given the code word and will tell it to you. The family code word is special and is not to be shared with friends. Your family code word is: _____

❑ It is a good idea for young teens to take First Aid, CPR, and certified baby-sitting courses from an agency such as the American Red Cross. These are important skills for both boys and girls.

SWIMMING

❑ Have your children learn to swim.

❑ Teach them not to swim alone.

❑ Do not go near water or swim without a parent or authorized adult's permission.

❑ Learn how to help someone else correctly. Taking classes in life-saving skills, First Aid, CPR, etc., should be encouraged.

❑ Never pretend to be "drowning" to distract lifeguards or other swimmers. They need to be watching for someone who might really be in trouble.

❑ Don't splash someone if they are uncomfortable with it and they have asked you not to.

❑ Never push or dunk someone under water.

❑ The sides of a pool are wet and slick; avoid running, pushing or playing rough near a pool. (Consider the preciousness of others and play in such a way that no one is needlessly hurt.)

❑ Avoid swimming directly in front of a diving board.

❑ Get out of a pool (or boat) during a thunder and lightening storm.

❑ Test the water temperature of hot tubs and spas before entering. They are often too hot for children. Little children can quickly become dangerously overheated. Even adults should be careful not to stay in them for an extended length of time; you may become weak and possibly faint.

❑ Do not submerge your head in an operating jetted tub. Your hair could get caught in the intake grill and you can be held under water.

❑ Be careful of strong under-tows in the ocean. The current can pull you under the water.

❑ Watch out for swift-moving water in rivers because it is moving faster and with more power than it shows on the surface.

❑ Look carefully for people or objects before you jump into water. Never dive head first into water when you cannot see the bottom, especially in natural bodies of water such as lakes, rivers, oceans, etc.

❑ When boating, always be familiar with the local laws, and always wear a life jacket.

❑ Do not stand up in a small boat or canoe.

❑ Remember, even good swimmers can drown, so be wise and be careful!

HIKING

❑ When preparing for a hike, check the weather forecast.

❑ Tell a friend or family member where you will be and when you will return. When you do get back, be sure to check in with them. In case you don't show up, they will assume you are having some trouble and they can organize help.

❑ Be prepared for the unexpected: Carry in your pack:
  • Plenty of fluids and food (like trail mix and beef jerky)
  • First aid items
  • Proper clothing, including something warm for rain, wind or cold weather
  • Warm hat
  • Thermal blanket
  • Good shoes
  • Map
  • Compass (and know how to use it)
  • Flashlight (and extra batteries and bulb)
  • Whistle
  • Multifunction pocketknife
  • Waterproof matches
  • If you hike frequently, consider purchasing a GPS unit (Global Positioning System)

❑ Stay on the marked hiking trails.

❑ Don't hike alone.

PLAYGROUNDS

❑ Keep clear of and away from swings when they are in use.

❑ If you are swinging and someone is waiting to take a turn, be kind and let him/her on in a reasonable amount of time.

❑ Don't climb up a slide when someone is sliding down. You'll be eating their shoes!

❑ Beware of metal slides on hot days. They can be very hot and cause serious burns.

❑ Be sure the last person is off the slide before you slide down.

❑ Never push or shove. Take turns on outdoor play equipment and wait in line patiently. Everyone will have more fun that way.

❑ Do not throw sand, gravel or sawdust in the air or at other children. This can cause eye injuries.

❑ If a ball goes into the street or parking lot, don't run out after it. Stop and check for traffic, then walk carefully to retrieve it. If a child is very young, an adult should go and get it.

❑ Use the public restrooms with parental permission only and preferably not alone.

PEDESTRIANS

❑ Wear light or bright clothing when walking at night (it helps during the day, too).

❑ Walk on the left side of the street, facing oncoming traffic.

❑ Watch for cars, motorcycles, bikes or any other moving vehicle. You may have the right of way, but they are still bigger than you!

❑ If it says, "Don't walk," then don't! Be patient! Wait at the corner for the "Walk" sign to come on. Always check to make sure all the cars have stopped, and then proceed.

❑ Before crossing the street look left, then right, then left again. Only proceed when it is truly safe. If still very young, only proceed while holding the hand of an adult.

❑ If you are in a group, cross together.

❑ Do not cross a street between parked cars.

❑ Stop, look and listen before crossing a railroad track. Do not climb over or under a train that is stopped on the track.

❑ When skating, skateboarding or in-line skating, wear safety gear: helmets, gloves, and knee and elbow pads. These can prevent or lessen injuries from falls. Do not skate in the street.

BIKES

You can also get information on bike safety from your local bike shop, but the following list may help:

❑ Always wear a helmet. Head injuries are permanent but preventable!

❑ Wear shoes when riding a bike.

❑ It is a good idea to have your children learn bicycle hand signals. Left arm extended straight out from your side means you are turning left. Extended left arm bent at the elbow and pointing up means you are turning right.

Extended left arm bent from the elbow and pointing down to the ground means you are going to stop.

❑ Don't ride double (side by side). Only ride in single file.

❑ Don't carry someone on your handlebars.

❑ Keep both hands on the handlebars, except when signaling.

❑ Keep to the right of the road and go in the same direction that cars are going. Ride in a straight line.

❑ Obey all traffic signals and signs. You are on a moving vehicle and subject to the same laws as a car.

❑ Walk your bike across busy intersections.

❑ Wear light-colored clothing that is easily seen at night (it helps during the day, too).

❑ Avoid riding at dusk when it is the most difficult to see a bike rider.

❑ Don't ride at night unless you have on light clothing, and your bike is equipped with good reflectors and a front headlight.

❑ Low-riding tricycles such as "Big Wheels" are too low to be seen by the driver of a car and should be used on sidewalks only.

❑ When riding on the sidewalk, be careful to watch for motor vehicles when crossing a driveway or alley.

❑ Be careful when riding past a car that is parallel parked. The driver may not have seen you and might open the car door into you.

MOTOR VEHICLES

Your Department of Motor Vehicles can provide you with motor vehicle safety tips. Your older teens can be enrolled in a driver's training program. Some of these suggestions can be shared with younger children.

❑ Always wear your safety belt.

❑ Do not move from your seat when the car or bus is in motion.

❑ Don't put any part of your body (head, legs, arms) outside a car or bus window.

❑ Avoid yelling or making sudden loud noises that can startle the driver.

❑ Do not throw toys, trash, or any other objects while *inside* a bus or car.

❑ Do not throw toys, trash, or any other objects *outside* of a bus or car.

❑ Avoid stowing unsecured cargo in the passenger areas of a vehicle. In a collision they can become dangerous flying projectiles.

❑ Do not pull on the arms, hands or legs of a driver.

❑ Do not ever handle any part of the steering column when an adult is not in the car.

❑ Do not ever touch or move the stick shift if you are not the driver.

❑ Do not attempt to start a car without being a licensed driver or a student with a driver's permit.

❑ Always get out of a car on the side closest to the curb if parallel parked.

❑ When riding a motorcycle, always wear a helmet and proper gear. Wear solid shoes, heavy long pants, long sleeves, and gloves. *Leather* is best.

- When riding a motorized go-cart or "mini-bike," dress like you would if you were riding a motorcycle (see above).

- Do not attempt to drive farm equipment unless you are supervised or are fully trained in its operation.

- When you are of age to drive a motor vehicle, always obey all traffic laws. Be mindful of signs, speed and the comfort and safety of passengers. Inexperience as well as "showing off" can cost lives – your passengers, other drivers and yourself. Be wise. Be careful.

- Never drive after having had alcoholic beverages (avoid these anyway), or strong medications (pain killers, and even antihistamines can hinder your driving ability). Let someone else drive for you or call someone to come and pick you up.

❑ Keep an emergency kit in the car. Include items such as:
  - Battery powered radio and flashlight and extra batteries
  - Emergency or personal cell phone
  - Blanket
  - Booster cables
  - Fire extinguisher
  - Bottled water
  - Non-perishable high energy foods
  - Maps
  - Shovel
  - Tire Gauge
  - Ice scraper
  - Chains
  - Tire puncture sealer
  - Duct tape
  - Phillips and slotted screw driver, pliers
  - Tow rope
  - Flare and/or reflective devices
  - First Aid kit

SHARP AND DANGEROUS THINGS

❑ Stay away from power tools or equipment unless an adult can supervise the activity (i.e. table saws, chain saws, lathes, etc.).

❑ Stay at a safe distance from power tools or equipment if they are being used by someone else.

❑ When using power equipment, use it for its intended purpose. For example, the lawn mower is to stay on the ground; it is not a hedge trimmer.

❑ Stay clear of lawn mowers being operated by someone else; they often kick up rocks and can send them flying.

❑ Do not leave power equipment running if you need to step away.

❑ Don't *ever* play with firearms (guns). As a parent, if you own firearms, it is your responsibility to teach your children proper respect for, and if appropriate, the use of firearms. Always keep them unloaded, locked up and put away from children.

❑ Do not play with firecrackers. Always use them under the direct supervision of an adult.

❑ Never re-light a "dud" (a firecracker that didn't go off); it could potentially explode in your hand.

❑ Never light a firecracker that you happen to find lying around.

❑ Know how to hold knives, scissors, or other sharp objects when walking: with the point down.

❑ If handing something sharp to someone, such as a knife or scissors, carefully give them the handle (not the blade).

❑ Keep fingers away from the garbage disposal.

ELECTRICITY

Although much of this is common knowledge for an adult, children need to be taught about electricity:

❑ Learn how to properly unplug an electrical appliance. Don't pull it out by the cord. Grasp the *plug* and gently pull. Make sure your hands are dry.

❑ Be careful not to overload outlets.

❑ Make sure electrical cords are not frayed and are in good condition before plugging them in.

❑ Never use appliances (i.e. hairdryers, toasters, etc.) near water, if you are wet or if you are standing in water. You could get seriously shocked.

❑ Before plugging in kitchen or workshop appliances (especially saws, blenders and mixers!), make sure they are in the *off* position.

❑ If toast gets stuck in the toaster, unplug the toaster *first*, and then try to get it out.

❑ Do not play behind the TV or the stereo system.

❑ Teach your older children where the breaker box is in your house and how to turn the household power off at the main switch.

❑ You may wish to teach how to turn on a tripped breaker or replace a blown fuse.

❑ When attempting to repair an electrical device, make sure the power is off.

❑ When replacing a light bulb, turn off the light at the switch.

❑ Do not touch someone being shocked; you will get shocked also. First and foremost, attempt to unplug the appliance or turn off the main switch at the breaker box. You can also use a long wooden stick (a broom handle), a dry rope or a long length of dry cloth to move the person away from the source of electricity. Check for signs of breathing or heartbeat. Call 911 and begin CPR if necessary.

❑ Look up before you climb a tree and check to make sure that there is no power line nearby or touching the tree. If there is, stay out of the tree.

❑ Never fly a kite, balloons or remote control airplanes near power lines. Fly them only in open areas.

❑ Stay far away from fallen power lines. They can arc and send out a current of electricity up to 15 feet away.

❑ If a power line falls across a car or bus, remain inside where it is safest. If you must leave the vehicle, *jump* away from it and land on *both* feet. Then shuffle away with baby steps and your feet touching together until you get at least 15 feet away from the power line. If someone tries to come near you to help, tell them to stay away and call 911.

❑ Always assume that a "down" power line or exposed wiring is "hot" (filled with electrical current).

HOT STUFF

❑ Teach little ones that ovens, stoves, lamps, radiators, woodstoves, irons, curling irons and barbecues are HOT!

❑ Stay away from outside barbecues during and after cooking. Remember that they stay hot for a *long* time after use.

❑ Do not lean against or touch wood-burning stoves when in use!

❑ Mufflers and tail pipes on motorized vehicles (as well as lawn mowers) are hot!

❑ Wear snug-fitting clothing (especially sleeves) when cooking so that you don't drag them across burners on the stove.

❏ Turn the handles of a pan toward the back of the stove (not over the burners) so that it does not get bumped and knocked over by someone walking by.

❏ Do not put plastic or paper bags on or near the stove or toaster.

❏ Let adults remove hot foods or liquids from the oven or stove.

❏ Use hot pads when removing foods from the microwave. Dishes can become very hot.

❏ Make sure you do not leave food on the stove unattended.

❏ Make sure the stove and oven are off when not in use.

❏ Let light bulbs cool before replacing them.

❏ Do not leave curlers, curling irons or pressing irons unattended. They can burn little fingers and even start a fire. Be sure to let them cool before putting them away.

FIRE

Consider the age and maturity level of your children when sharing the following information. You do not want to frighten little children with too much information.

❏ Learn to STOP, DROP, and ROLL (to extinguish fire on body or clothing).

❏ Don't smoke!

❏ Don't play with lighters or matches! They are tools for specific purposes and are not to be considered "toys." Older children should be instructed in how to use them safely and then only under the supervision of a parent or responsible adult.

❏ Do not "roughhouse" around an open campfire, wood stove or fireplace.

❑ Extinguish a campfire if it will be left unattended.

❑ Keep toys and clothing articles away from space heaters, baseboard or wall heaters.

❑ Learn how to extinguish a grease fire with baking soda or a pan lid. Never use water or attempt to carry the pan outside, you'll only feed and spread the flames.

❑ Learn how to use a fire extinguisher (keep one or more in the house). Make sure they are fully charged and operational.

❑ Install smoke alarms on each level of your house and in the garage. Keep one in each bedroom, in every hallway and living area.

❑ Learn how to check smoke alarms monthly and make sure they are in good operating order. Replace batteries at least once every year (without fail!)

❑ Know how to escape from a house fire. Crawl and keep low to the floor to avoid the smoke. Feel doors and doorknobs and see if they are hot. If they are, do not enter the room. Go another way. Each room should have two planned ways of escape.

❑ Remember that smoke as well as fire can kill – stay low!

❑ Learn how to use an escape ladder for second story houses.

❑ Never take an elevator during a fire. If the power goes out, you will be stuck in a burning building. Always take the stairs.

❑ Plan a specific place where you are to meet outside if there is a fire, and stay there! Do not take things with you. Your life is the only thing of real value!

❑ *Never, never, never* re-enter a burning building.

❑ Practice fire drills with your children.

❑ Instruct your children to make emergency calls to the fire department during a fire (911) from the *neighbor's* house, not their own.

ANIMALS

❑ Don't poke fingers through fences or cages. You may get bitten!

❑ Don't feed wild animals; they can bite you and they can carry diseases such as rabies.

❑ If tempted to pick up a reptile or insect, be sure that you are not in an area where they are poisonous. If it could be poisonous, it would be wise to leave it alone! If you are bitten, seek medical attention immediately.

❑ Never approach an animal when it is eating; never attempt to take its food away.

❑ Do not approach an unfamiliar dog. Never pet strange or sick-looking animals, whether they are wild or domestic.

❑ Always approach a *friend's* dog slowly and from the side (that is how dogs approach each other). Take your time and let the dog check you out. When he seems to accept you, then pet him.

❑ When a dog growls and bares his teeth, he is warning you to stay away. It is the only language he has. Leave him alone.

❑ If a dog growls at you, stand still with your hands to your sides and don't look into the dog's eyes. The dog will usually lose interest and go away. If he doesn't, talk in a soothing manner. If he seems to accept you, walk toward the dog, past it and away. Never move quickly or run. And do not pet the dog.

❑ If you are attacked by a dog, throw your arms in front of your face. If you get knocked down, curl up, roll on your stomach and protect your head and neck with your arms. Then lie still.

❑ Never, ever attempt to physically break up a dog or a cat fight. You will be the loser!

❑ When a cat or dog (or any animal with teeth, beak or claws) wants down and out of your arms, put them down or you will find yourself bitten or scratched.

❑ Treat all animals with kindness and gentleness. Do not tease, hit, kick or toss them.

STRANGERS

This is a difficult area to teach and yet it is very important to teach it often. Be careful not to instill fear in a child, but do instill wisdom and caution. Many of the following rules can be acted out and role-played as a family, so that a child can have the boldness to say, "NO" loudly and with confidence. You might even want to consider a class on self-defense for children (or yourself). None of the following things will probably happen to your children, but it is still very important for them to know what to do – just in case. *Much of the following information is written for you as if you were speaking directly to your children about these issues:*

❑ A stranger is someone you don't know. Even if they look nice or act friendly, they are still strangers unless your parents know their names and have gotten to know them well. Even neighbors you don't know must be considered strangers until your parents have met them.

❑ Most strangers are good people, but some are not. Bad people can act gentle, friendly and nice. They can be dressed in nice clothes, too. Don't be fooled! A stranger is a stranger.

❑ Do not go with a stranger if they want to show you something (new kittens, new furniture, etc.). If they want to show you something, they should ask your parents for permission.

❑ Do not help a stranger if they ask for it. Adults don't need help from children. Do not help give them directions, look for a lost puppy, etc. Adults should ask other *adults* for help.

❑ If you think a stranger really does need assistance, go get an adult or call 911.

❑ If a stranger in a car stops to talk to you or offers you candy, (or asks you to look at his puppies or kittens, or anything else) do not go up to the car. Quickly get away from the person and notify a parent or responsible adult immediately. Tell them everything you remember: the way the person looked, the color of the car, which way they went...etc.

❑ Do not get into a car if someone says your parents are in trouble and they will take you to them. Parents in difficult situations will notify authorities and keep you informed through familiar channels. Strangers will not be sent, unless they were from the sheriff's department or the police, and they will be in uniform *and* have a marked vehicle.

❑ Remember your family code word, so that if your parents do send someone to get you, he will have been given the code word and will tell it to you. If he doesn't know it, *do not go with them no matter what he says!* Your family code word is: _____

❑ Even if it is pouring down rain and you are walking home from school, do not get in a stranger's car if he offers you a ride home.

❑ Never go for a walk with a stranger or get into a stranger's car for any reason!! Immediately run and tell an adult if someone asks you to. If someone tries to force you to go with him somewhere, yell loudly, "You're not my father (or mother)!" Then quickly get away.

❑ If someone does grab you and attempts to force you to go with him, *keep your thinking clear.* One of your best defenses is to scream loud and long, and keep on screaming. Biting, hitting and kicking (the knee, shin, groin, and sensitive other places) are also helpful. Do you best to get away and then run quickly to a safe place. Notify the police immediately and give them the best description you can.

❑ *Never, ever* hitchhike.

❑ Do not go to public places alone (especially to the bathroom). Always have a buddy (someone to go with you). The buddy system is always a wise idea.

❑ When you go to the bathroom away from home, go in pairs or with an adult you trust. Do your business and leave. A bathroom is not a good place to play.

❑ Do not go alone into a deserted place such as an empty park, forested area or abandoned building.

❑ If you *must* go somewhere alone, walk quickly with confidence and your head held up. Keep your wits about you and be aware of your surroundings. Do not take short cuts through paths off the main road.

❑ If you see a stranger hanging around a school playground, in the park, or other place where children are present, go and tell an adult. He may be waiting to harm children.

❑ If a stranger asks to take your picture, say, "No thank you." Then leave and tell your parents or a responsible adult right away.

❑ If you see a stranger in a school bathroom, leave right away and tell your teacher.

❑ Always tell your parents where you are going whenever you leave the house. Even if you are simply leaving the yard or wish to go to a friend's house, ask your parents for permission. It is your parents' job to know where you are.

❑ If you are home alone and you answer the phone, never admit to being alone. Tell them, "My Mom can't get to the phone right now. May I take a message and have her call you back?" Or better yet, just let an answering machine answer the calls. You can hear the speaker's voice and answer it if it really is someone you want to talk to.

❑ If you are arriving home alone, have your house key out and ready to use, then be sure to lock the door behind you. If someone is lurking nearby, or something looks suspicious, such as a broken window, do not go in. Go to a trusted neighbor's house or the closest phone and call 911. Then call your parent or trusted adult.

❑ When you are home alone, make sure the doors and windows are locked.

❑ If you are accidentally left home alone by a parent (this has been known to happen) have an emergency plan in place: First, stop and pray. Ask God to help you remain calm and make the correct decisions. Second, know whom you are to call (i.e. other parent, grandparent, neighbor, etc.). Third, remain at home (unless given other instructions). Read a book or watch TV patiently. Finally, relax. It probably won't be long before your parent realizes their mistake and comes back to get you!

❑ If you are accidentally separated from your parents in a crowd (a store, mall, fair, etc.), have an agreed upon place where you can meet and get back together again. For instance, at a mall, you can meet at the information booth (most malls have these) or you can remain in the store where you last saw your parents. Let a store clerk (usually someone with a name tag or uniform) know you are lost, and stay with them. Many stores have an intercom they can use to call for your parents. If you are at a public event, such as at a fair, either go to an information or ticket booth, or remain at the exhibit where you last saw your parents. Do not attempt to wander around looking for your parents, this will only prolong their search. Do not go to the parking lot looking for your parent's car; this is not a safe place for children to be wandering around. (*Parents, plan your meeting place each time you go to a public area so that everyone will know what to do, and where to go. In this way, everyone is acting with thought and reason and no one will need to panic.)*

❑ If you are home alone and a stranger comes to the door, do not open the door or let him in, even if he has a uniform on. If it is a man or woman who says they are the police, there should be a marked police car with them. If there isn't, ask them to wait, dial 911 and ask if a policeman was sent to your address. If it is a delivery person and he has a delivery, ask him to leave it at the door and wait until he drives away before you open the door and bring it inside. (Keep in mind the age of your child when teaching this.)

❑ If you make a mistake and do answer the door and you are alone, don't let the caller know you are by yourself. Tell them your parent is "busy right now."

❑ If a stranger keeps ringing or knocking on the door, call a neighbor or the police to check on him.

❑ Go to a trusted neighbor's house if you ever feel uncomfortable or if something strange happens when you are alone.

❑ If you feel you are nearing a dangerous place or situation, leave immediately.

❑ If you see anybody of any age displaying a gun for any reason, leave and notify a responsible adult immediately.

❑ If someone tries to steal your purse or other possession, let him have it. Your personal safety is far more important than money or things.

❑ If you are of driving age, always check the front and back seat of your car before you get in and immediately lock your car once inside.

❑ When parking your car at night, always park in a well-lit area as close to the building as possible. When returning to your car, ask for a trusted escort to walk with you if the parking lot is vacant or you feel uncomfortable.

❑ Keep sufficient gas in your car, and keep it in good running order so that you do not have unnecessary breakdowns on the road.

❑ Beware of car-jackings. If someone bumps your car and you feel suspicious, drive to a well-lit place of business to exchange insurance information.

TOUCHING

This is another subject that is very difficult to teach. To even have to speak of "touching" seems to violate the innocence and purity of children. However, children need to be equipped to protect themselves as best they can from those in our society who would seek to harm them. The following points are general concepts for you as parents to consider and then teach to your children. Keep in mind, "touching" in the context of this discussion refers to physical contact with a child's private areas.

❑ Private areas are the parts of the body that are covered by a bathing suit. They are not ugly, shameful or bad. Rather, they are precious and beautiful for they have been created by our loving God for a very special purpose. It is God's desire that we protect them carefully and cover them modestly.

❑ Children need to be taught to respect other people's bodies. It is normal to be curious, but it is not right to look at or play games that involve someone else's private areas. Let your child know that they may ask you their questions about bodies and that you will always answer them the best way that you can, and that you will not make light of their questions. (Be careful when answering their questions to give them information that is appropriate for their age and that will keep their minds pure.)

❑ To prevent confusion, children need to understand that there are two types of touching: that which is *normal* and that which is *wrong*.

Normal Touching:

This is touching that takes place in the normal events of everyday life and involves parents, grandparents, baby-sitters, day-care providers, or other persons who care for your children. It is normal touching when:

☐ A child needs a diaper changed or needs help putting on underclothes or swimwear.

☐ A child is being bathed, dried off, or dressed.

☐ A child needs help cleaning himself after using the bathroom.

☐ A child has a medical problem in their private area that needs attention from a doctor, parent, or caregiver.

☐ A child is having a normal physical examination from a doctor or medical practitioner. (Often in the medical profession, a conscientious doctor will perform these examinations while a nurse or parent is present in the room to avoid any problems.)

☐ A child is given a playful pat on the bottom.

☐ A child is receiving chastisement (a spanking) on the bottom. (No bare bottoms, please. It is important, even in discipline, to respect your child's dignity.)

Wrong Touching:

These are touches that do not feel "normal." Wrong touches can come from a person of any age, man or woman, stranger, friend, or relative. These touches go beyond the "normal" as mentioned above, and they go beyond childhood curiosity. These types of touches are a violation of a child's private body. Very often children can tell if the touching is wrong. A little alarm goes off in their heads that tells them that this is different, it doesn't feel right, and they are uncomfortable. A child can know it is *wrong* touching when:

☐ A person, who may or may not be a stranger, offers money, candy or toys to touch, play with, or see the child's private areas.

❑ A person touches their private areas and tells the child that it is their "special secret." Adults should never ask a child to keep a "special secret" about touching. Children do not have to keep those kinds of "secrets."

❑ A person touches a child's private areas and does not stop. Perhaps insisting that a child sit on their lap without letting them get down.

❑ A person touches a child's private areas and then threatens to hurt the child or her parents if they tell. Explain to the child that the person is only trying to scare her. It is important that she comes and tells anyway.

❑ Children can be taught a helpful "tool" that will remind them what to do if they get into this kind of difficult situation. This tool is three simple words that remind them of three actions to take: *NO – GO – TELL*.

NO: A child can say "No" if he is being touched in a way that is wrong.

GO: A child should quickly leave a situation if he feels that something wrong is happening.

TELL: If a child has been touched in a wrong way, he needs to go and tell someone right away.

Discuss with your children who they can trust and talk to if necessary. (If they have told someone and they did not get help, then they should tell someone else until an adult does something about the problem.)

❑ Telling is very difficult for a child to do because they often feel shame and embarrassment over what happened; in fact, they may even feel responsible. They may be so upset or confused that they keep the event all to themselves. It is very important that you teach your children that if someone does touch them in a wrong way, *it is not their fault*. They need to know that they can and should come and tell you what happened, and that you will listen and help them.

❑ If something has happened, do not panic. The child needs to feel safe and secure and know that you are in control. Let the child know that you will do whatever is necessary to help them, protect them, and take care of the situation. It is important that corrective steps be taken quickly and that the situation not be allowed to rest. A person with a touching problem needs to be stopped and will need help in stopping. If the perpetrator does not get help, the problem will continue, not just with your child, but possibly with someone else's as well.

...so just remember,
teach a child to tell,
listen if they tell,
and if they tell,
do something about it.

Epilogue

As you can see, there is quite a lot to teach and impress upon the hearts and minds of your children. And these lists are by no means complete. There will always be more that you will want to include, modify and adapt to fit your own unique family situation.

It is my hope that the previous pages will serve as a helpful tool in your parenting and training process. May it give you a sense of direction and confidence in your purpose.

May the principles of God's Word guide you each step of the way as you endeavor to raise children who love the Lord and want to live virtuous and useful lives in obedience and service to Him. And may your prayers on their behalf be unceasingly presented before the throne of God.

As parents we must seek to abide in the Lord and do our very best in His strength. Ultimately, when children leave home they will make their own choices in life. Pray that the choices they make will be in keeping with the Scriptural principles that you have faithfully taught. May they honor you with their lives and rise up and call you blessed.

Galatians 6:9: Let us not become weary in doing good,
for at the proper time we will reap a harvest
if we do not give up.

Resources

There are *so many* excellent and helpful resources available on the raising of children, that it is almost a disservice to list some here. Please use this list as a starting point and further explore the multitudes of other helpful and creative materials that are equally deserving of mention. Christian bookstores will be a valuable source of help, as will church and local libraries.

PARENTING
Ezzo, Gary & Anne Marie. *Growing Kids God's Way.* The founders of the ministry, *Growing Families International*, are Gary and Anne Marie Ezzo. Over the years they have developed and authored parenting curricula used around the world. They lay a biblical foundation for parenting which seeks to train the heart of the child, rather than just conforming outward behavior.

Growing Families International
Customer Service
PO Box 54
Louisiana, MO 63353
1-800-474-6264

Trumbull, Clay H. *Hints on Child Training.* Eugene: Great Expectations Book Co., 1990. A newly updated book of practical parenting principles that stand the test of time.

Decker, Barbara; *Proverbs for Parenting.* Boise: Lynn's Bookshelf, 1991. A topical guide for child raising from the Book of Proverbs.

Hadidian, Allen & Connie and Wilson, Will & Lindy. *Creative Family Times.* Chicago: Moody Press, 1989. Truly creative ideas that make raising children purposeful and fun. These ideas are easy to implement and benefit both parent and child.

Bennet, William J., ed. *The Book of Virtues*. New York: Simon & Schuster, 1983. A compilation of short stories, poetry and selected articles, organized according to virtuous character qualities. This book sparks thoughtful conversations that challenge both parent and child. This book is thoroughly enjoyable by children of all ages.

Doorposts. This company produces Bible-based books, charts and other products that help you apply scripture in your home.

Doorposts
5905 SW Lookingglass Drive
Gaston, OR 97119
503-357-4749
www.doorposts.net

Suggestion: Reading biographies of great Christians, be they missionaries or otherwise, can become a wonderful source of inspiration. Great discussions and even a child's life direction can be inspired when these are read individually or as a family. Biographies such as these are available through most sources of Christian materials.

DEVOTIONAL MATERIALS
Baker, Dr. Donald & Mary. *Bible Study Guide For All Ages*. Clarksville: B.S.B. Printing, 1982. A four volume set that takes the family through a serious study of the scriptures. Includes continuous review, memory work, and a chronological time-line.

Elwell, Marty. *Searching for Treasure*. Gresham: Noble Publishing Assoc., 1993. A guide to wisdom and character development. Written for the whole family to study, and enjoy together.

Jahsmann, Allan H. and Simon, Martin P. *Little Visits with God*. Saint Louis: Concordia, 1960. A book of devotions for families with young children. Each chapter contains a scenario that teaches a lesson, followed with scripture, questions and prayer. Children love the stories.

Schoolland, Marian M. *Leading Little Ones to God*. Grand Rapids: Wm. B. Eerdmans, 1962. Systematic theology simplified for children. An excellent teaching tool on the fundamentals of the faith.

Taylor, Kenneth N. *Wise Words for Little People*. Wheaton: Tyndale House Publishers, Inc., 1971. This book, along with the others in this series, *Big Thoughts for Little People*, and *Giant Steps for Little People*, are precious devotions for young children. Scripture is applied to real situations that children can understand and are accompanied by delightful illustrations. Meaningful, fun and well loved by children.

Walk Thru the Bible Study Guides. There are many study aids to choose from. To receive a catalog, write:

Walk Thru the Bible Ministries®
4201 North Peachtree Road
Atlanta, GA 30341
or call: 1 (800)868-9300

Weed, Libby., ed. *Read-n-Grow Picture Bible*. Fort Worth: Sweet Publishing, 1984. Bible stories in comic book form. Fun to read to children and fun for them to read on their own.

BIBLE STUDY HELPS FOR THE FAMILY LIBRARY
Bible Concordance – with Hebrew and Greek Dictionaries
Bible Commentaries
Bible Dictionary
Bible Atlas
Church History
Good Historical Time Line (beginning at creation)
Hymnals

There are many of these resources available by different authors. You may want to spend time evaluating and comparing them before you make a purchase.

PRACTICAL SKILLS AND HOME MANAGEMENT

American Red Cross. Check out your local chapter where you will find excellent resources on safety, first aid, and emergency preparedness.

Aslett, Don. *Do I Dust or Vacuum First?* Cincinnati: C.J. Krehbiel Co., 1987. This is a very helpful book with tips on how, when and why to clean things the right way. I would highly recommend any book by Don Aslett. He is humorous and informative.

Campbell, Jeff. *Speed Cleaning*. New York: Bantam, 1987. This is a delightful book of time saving ideas to make house cleaning as efficient as possible.

McCullough, Bonnie Runyan and Monson, Susan Walker. *401 Ways to Get Your Children to Work at Home*. New York: Saint Martin's Press, 1981. Great ideas to motivate your kids!

Mendelson, Cheryl. *Home Comforts: The Art and Science of Keeping House*. New York: Scribner, 1999. This book is a fascinating, comprehensive treasure trove of invaluable information that restores the art of keeping house.

Rombauer, Irma S., Rombauer Becker, Marion. *The Joy of Cooking*. New York: Scribner, 1995. This is a wonderfully thorough cook book that not only includes wonderful recipes but also illustrates and explains cooking technique. A classic.

Young, Pam and Jones, Peggy. *Sidetracked Home Executives*. New York: Warner, 1983. As this humorous and helpful book says, "Two successful sisters tell you how they moved from "pigpen to paradise" from clutter and chaos to order – and how easily you can do it too!

For additional resources: Use your church or local library and check out books, tapes and videos on such topics as: Manners, Character, Courtship, Safety, Bible Lands, Church History, Bible Stories, Christian Music, Sacred Hymns, Home Management, Fun Family Activities, and more.

Wishing you years of family learning, growing, and fun!